leopold stokowski

second edition of
the discography
compiled by
john hunt

Acknowledgement

These publications have been made possible by contributions or advance subscriptions from

Richard Ames
Yoshihiro Asada
Michael Bral*
Jonathan Brown
Edward Chibas*
Dennis Davis
Hans-Peter Ebner*
Nobuo Fukumoto
Philip Goodman*
Johann Gratz*
Michael Harris*
Naoya Hirabayashi
E.M. Johnson
Koji Kinoshita
J-F. Lambert*
Douglas MacIntosh*
Carlo Marinelli*
Bruce Morrison*
Alan Newcombe*
Jim Parsons*
David Patmore*
James Pearson
Mavis Robinson
Ingo Schwarz
John Shackleton
Yoshihiko Suzuki*
Urs Weber*
Nigel Wood*
Ken Wyman
Stefano Angeloni*
J.M. Blyth*
Marc Bridle
Brian Capon
Robert Dandois
John Derry
Henry Fogel*
Peter Fülop*
Jean-Pierre Goossens
Alan Haine
Tadashi Hasegawa*
Bodo Igesz
Rodney Kempster*
Detlef Kissmann*
Elisabeth Legge-Schwarzkopf*
John Mallinson*
Philip Moores*
W. Moyle
Hugh Palmer*
Laurence Pateman*
J.A. Payne
Tully Potter
Yutaka Sasaki*
Tom Scragg*
Robert Simmons*
Michael Tanner
John Welson
Graeme Wright*

*indicates life subscriber

STOKOWSKI conducts BEETHOVEN

Symphonies Nos. 5 and 7

Historic Recordings with

THE PHILADELPHIA ORCHESTRA

the LEOPOLD STOKOWSKI society

LS 13

Leopold Stokowski/1882-1977: an introduction to the discography

When I last surveyed the recorded legacy of Leopold Stokowski, the record market was rapidly heading for a predicted close-down. New recordings by serious classical artists were becoming few and far between, both in quantity and quality, and re-issues of back catalogue were deemed to be of minority interest and frankly unmarketable, leaving the field open for unofficial editions which were sometimes of dubious quality.

To the surprise of many, therefore, the demand for great performances from the past has grown and diversified in the last decade, with care taken over transfers which can be of remarkable quality and fidelity to the original sound. Labels like Dutton, Andante, Pearl, Biddulph and Cala have taken over to a significant extent from the major companies in preserving legacies, supplemented in the case of Stokowski by a number of enthusiasts who are publishing private editions (on a non-commercial basis) of previously unavailable live performances. These collectors are in possession of much more recorded Stokowski material as yet unpublished, including war-time concerts with the NBC Symphony, performances at the Hollywood Bowl in 1945-1946, and countless concerts (and rehearsals) from the later years with the American Symphony Orchestra.

It is this activity among Stokowski collectors world-wide that accounts for the considerable expansion of this printed discography, to the extent that the planned up-date of Stokowski's concert activity has had to be put aside for a later separate volume.

An aspect of the discography which will strike the newcomer to Stokowski's work will be the inclusion of many a musical wotk not normally associated with the modern symphony orchestra. These are of course the famous Stokowski transcriptions, a category which embraces not only those numerous and well-known arrangements of Bach choral and instrumental pieces, through piano pieces by Beethoven, Chopin, Mozart, Rachmaninov, Scriabin and Tchaikovsky, but also extends to transcriptions from opera in both vocal and non-vocal versions. In common with most active musicians of Stokowski's own or earlier generations (Gustav Mahler, Willem Mengelberg, Arturo Toscanini, Henry Wood), he would also "re-touch" many standard classical works, an acknowledged practice in at least the first half of the twentieth century. The need for special high-lighting of these arrangements when listing Stokowski's recordings has not therefore been deemed necessary.

the
LEOPOLD
STOKOWSKI
society

SAINT-SAËNS

Scenes from

SAMSON AND DELILAH

RISË STEVENS

JAN PEERCE

ROBERT MERRILL

N.B.C. SYMPHONY ORCHESTRA

and the

ROBERT SHAW CHORALE

Conducted by

LEOPOLD STOKOWSKI

10th
ANNIVERSARY
ISSUE
1979-1989

A particularly welcome improvement in this second edition of my Stokowski discography is the inclusion wherever possible of precise recording dates, rather than just month and year which was previously given. Opportunity was also taken to correct previous errors. I have also endeavoured to include the versions of musical works made by Stokowski for the various motion pictures in which he participated (the previous discography included only the material featured in *Fantasia* and *Carnegie Hall*).

Collectors who wish to investigate the privately issued Stokowski material mentioned above are referred to the respective websites which can be found on the internet. Of these, I am particularly indebted to Theo van der Burg and Enno Riekena, to whose listings I have constantly referred. Further help came from Michael Gray, Bill Holland, Robert Stumpf and Malcolm Walker, and from Dennis Davis of the Leopold Stokowski Society.

ISBN 1 901395 19 7
Printed by Short Run Press, Exeter

the LEOPOLD STOKOWSKI society
Stokowski conducts Wagner
"Tannhäuser" Overture and Venusberg Music · Prelude to Act 3
"Tristan and Isolde" Symphonic Synthesis
Leopold Stokowski and his Symphony Orchestra

ADOLPHE ADAM (1803-1856)

giselle, selection from the ballet suite

new york 16 may 1950	his symphony orchestra	78: victor M 1394 45: victor WDM 1394 lp: victor LM 1083/VIC 1020 lp: hmv ALP 1133 lp: electrola WALP 1133 cd: kenwest (usa) 605 cd: theo van der burg (netherlands)

ISAAC ALBENIZ (1860-1909)

fete-dieu a séville/ibéria

philadelphia 27 september 1928	philadelphia orchestra	78: victor 7158 78: hmv D 1888 cd: biddulph WHL 047 cd: pearl GEMMCD 9276
new york 9 january 1944	nbc symphony	unpublished recording
new york 1 december 1962	american symphony	unpublished rehearsal recording
west ham july 1976	national philharmonic	lp: cbs 34543/73589 cd: cala CACD 0529

HUGO ALFVEN (1872-1960)

swedish rhapsody no 1

los angeles 25 august 1946	hollywood bowl symphony	cd: enno riekena (germany) *this is an abridged version of the rhapsody*

DANIELE AMFITHEATROV (1901-1983)

de profundis clamavi

new york 20 february 1944	nbc symphony	unpublished recording

russian march

los angeles 18 august 1946	hollywood bowl symphony	unpublished recording

FIRKET AMIROV (1922-1984)

kurd ovshari, symphonic mugam

houston 18 march 1959	houston symphony	lp: everest LPBR 3032/SDBR 3032 cd: pantheon D 1032X cd: everest EVC 9048
new york 5 march 1960	new york philharmonic	unpublished recording

GEORGE ANTHEIL (1900-1959)

symphony no 4

new york 13 february 1944	nbc symphony	cd: cala CACD 0528

over the plains

los angeles 4 august 1946	hollywood bowl symphony	unpublished recording

JACOB AVSHALOMOV (born 1919)

evocations for clarinet and orchestra

new york 22 february 1953	cbs studio orchestrra tishman, clarinet	cd: enno riekena (germany)

JOHANN SEBASTIAN BACH (1685-1750)

adagio from the organ toccata, adagio and fugue in c

camden nj 28 october 1933	philadelphia orchestra	78: victor M 236/M 243 78: hmv DB 2335 cd: pearl GEMMCDS 9098 cd: grammofono AB 78782 cd: history 20.3290 cd: membran 222174
new york 6 december 1942	nbc symphony	unpublished recording
new york 29 december 1971	american symphony	unpublished recording
new york 1 march 1972	american symphony	unpublished recording

air from the third suite

philadelphia 15 january 1936	philadelphia orchestra	78: victor M 401 78: hmv DA 1605 cd: pearl GEMMCDS 9098 cd: grammofono AB 78782 cd: history 20.3290 cd: membran 222174 cd: cantus classics 500.150 cd: allegro CDO 1011
new york 11 july 1941	all-american symphony	78: columbia (usa) X 220 cd: cala CACD 0527
new york 26 may 1958	his symphony orchestra	lp: capitol P 8458/SP 8458/SP 8650 lp: emi SXLP 30174 cd: emi CDM 769 0722/CDM 565 9122/ 566 3852/574 0492 cd: theo van der burg (netherlands)
new york 19 may 1968	american symphony	unpublished recording *recording apparently also made at rehearsal*
london 16-19 april 1974	london symphony	lp: rca ARL1-0880/AGL1-3656/ GL 42921/VL 42054 cd: rca/bmg 09026 612672/09026 626052/ 09026 684432
vence 22 july 1975	rouen chamber orchestra	unpublished recording *recording made at stokowski's final conducting appearance*

bach/**andante from violin sonata no 3**

new york 11 july 1941	all-american symphony	78: columbia (usa) X 541 cd: music and arts CD 845 cd: cala CACD 0527

arioso from cantata no 156

new york 11 july 1941	all-american symphony	78: columbia (usa) X 541 cd: cala CACD 0527
new york 25 november 1942	nbc symphony	unpublished recording
new york 27 november 1942	nbc symphony	78: victor 18498 78: hmv DB 6150 cd: biddulph BID 83069-83070
new york 29 december 1971	american symphony	unpublished recording
london 18-19 april 1974	london symphony	lp: rca ARL1-0880/AGM1-3656/ GL 42921/VL 42054 cd: rca/bmg 09026 612672/09026 626052/ 74321 709312

aus der tiefe rufe ich, chorale prelude

camden nj 15 march 1930	philadelphia orchestra	78: victor 7553 78: hmv DB 1789 lp: dell' arte DA 9001 cd: pearl GEMMCDS 9098 cd: grammofono AB 78782

bach/**bourrée from english suite no 2**

philadelphia 13-15 january 1936	philadelphia orchestrra	lp: neiman marcus (usa) cd: pearl GEMMCDS 9098 *unpublished victor 78rpm recording, although it was allocated catalogue number DA 1639 by hmv*
new york 24 march 1950	his symphony orchestra	78: victor M 1512 45: victor ERA 69 lp: victor LM 1133 lp: hmv ALP 1387/BLP 1074 lp: rca AGM1-5280 cd: rca/bmg GD 60922 cd: archipel ARPCD 0056
new york 5-11 february 1958	his symphony orchestra	lp: capitol P 8489/SP 8489 lp: emi MFP 2062 cd: emi CDM 769 0722/566 3852/ 574 0492 *recording completed on 26 february 1958*

brandenburg concerto no 2

philadelphia 27-29 september 1928	philadelphia orchestra	78: victor M 59 78: hmv D 1708-1710/D 7420-7422 78: hmv (france) W 1061-1063 78: electrola EJ 504-506 cd: andante 1986
new york 12 december 1943	nbc symphony	unpublished recording

brandenburg concerto no 4

new york 23 october 1966	american symphony	unpublished recording *recording apparently also made at rehearsal*

brandenburg concerto no 5

philadelphia 25 february 1960	philadelphia orchestrra valenti, harpsichord brusilov, violin kincaid, flute	lp: columbia (usa) ML 5713/MS 6313/Y-33228 lp: cbs 30061 cd: sony MH2K 62345

bach/**chaconne from violin partita no 2**

camden nj 30 april 1934	philadelphia orchestra	78: victor M 243 78: hmv DB 2541-2543 cd: pearl GEMMCDS 9098
new york 25 april 1950	his symphony orchestra	78: victor M 1512 lp: victor LM 1133 lp: rca AGM1-5280 cd: rca/bmg GD 60922 cd: archipel ARPCD 0056
chicago 2 january 1958	chicago symphony	unpublished recording
new york 8 may 1970	american symphony	unpublished recording
london 7 january 1974	london symphony	unpublished recording
london 16-19 april 1974	london symphony	lp: rca ARL1-0880/AGL1-3656/ GL 42921/VL 42054 cd: rca/bmg 09026 612672/09026 626052/ 09026 684432

christ lag in todesbanden, chorale prelude

camden nj 4 april 1931	philadelphia orchestra	78: victor 7437 78: hmv DB 1952 cd: pearl GEMMCDS 9098 cd: history 20.3290 cd: grammofono AB 78782 cd: allegro CDO 1011 cd: membran 222174
new york 12 december 1943	nbc symphony	unpublished recording

bach/**concerto in d minor for keyboard and orchestra**

new york 24 november 1969	american symphony read, harpsichord	unpublished recording

concerto in c minor for 4 keyboards and orchestra

los angeles 4 august 1945	hollywood bowl symphony lohmann, lewin, eustis, chang, pianos	unpublished recording

ein' feste burg ist unser gott, chorale prelude

camden nj 28 october 1933	philadelphia orchestra	78: victor 1692 78: hmv DB 2453 cd: music and arts CD 1173 *abbreviated version which was later replaced by april 1939 recording but using same catalogue number*
philadelphia 1936	philadelphia orchestra	film soundtrack recording *the big broadcast of 1937*
philadelphia 20 april 1939	philadelphia orchestra	78: victor 1692 cd: pearl GEMMCDS 9098
new york 4 july 1941	all-american symphony	78: columbia (usa) X 219/12903 cd: cala CACD 0527
new york 7 april 1942	nbc symphony	unpublished recording
rome 30 april 1955	rai roma orchestra	unpublished recording
new york 5-11 february 1958	his symphony	lp: capitol P 8489/P 8694/SP 8489/ SP 8694 lp: emi MFP 2062 lp: angel seraphim 60235 cd: emi CDM 769 0722/566 3852/ 574 0492 *recording completed on 26 february 1958*
london 7 january 1974	london symphony	unpublished recording
london 16-19 april 1974	london symphony	lp: rca ARL1-0880/AGL1-3656/ GL 42921/VL 42054 cd: rca/bmg 09026 612672/09026 626052/ 09026 684432

bach/**es ist vollbracht/johannes-passion**

camden nj 22 october 1934	philadelphia orchestra	78: victor 8764 78: hmv DB 2762 cd: music and arts CD 1173
philadelphia 8 december 1940	philadelphia orchestra	78: victor M 963 cd: pearl GEMMCDS 9098 cd: history 20.3290 cd: grammofono AB 78782 cd: allegro CDO 1011 cd: membran 222174
new york 28 march 1943	nbc symphony	unpublished recording
philadelphia 6 february 1962	philadelphia orchestra	unpublished recording

first movement from trio sonata no 1

philadelphia 27 november 1939	philadelphia orchestra	78: victor M 963 78: hmv DB 6260 cd: pearl GEMMCDS 9098
new york 29 december 1971	american symphony	unpublished recording

fugue in c minor/wohltemperiertes klavier book 1

camden nj 7 april 1934	philadelphia orchestra	78: victor 1985/M 243 78: hmv DB 2453 lp: rca camden CAL 120 cd: pearl GEMMCDS 9098 *rca camden lp described performers as warwick symphony orchestra*
new york 7 may 1966	american symphony	cd: theo van der burg (netherlands) *this was a rehearsal performance*

bach/**ich ruf' zu dir herr jesu christ, chorale prelude**

philadelphia 13 october 1927	philadelphia orchestra	78: victor 6786/M 530 78: hmv D 1464 lp: neiman marcus (usa) lp: dell' arte DA 9001 cd: pearl GEMMCDS 9098
philadelphia 27 november 1939	philadelphia orchestra	78: victor M 963 cd: music and arts CD 1173
new york 1944	new york city symphony	unpublished recording
new york 20 february 1949	new york philharmonic	lp: new york philharmonic NYP 821-822 cd: theo van der burg (netherlands)
rome 30 april 1955	rai roma orchestra	unpublished recording
philadelphia 25 february 1960	philadelphia orchestra	lp: columbia (usa) ML 5713/MS 6313/ MGP 17/Y-33228 lp: cbs 30061 cd: sony MH2K 62345
philadelphia 6 februaty 1962	philadelphia orchestra	unpublished recording
new york 3-5 october 1963	american symphony	unpublished rehearsal recording

jauchzet frohlocket!/weihnachtsoratorium

new york 18-20 december 1965	american symphony and chorus	unpublished recording
new york 29 december 1971	american symphony and chorus	unpublished recording

bach/**jesu bleibet meine freude/cantata no 147**

new york	his symphony	78: victor 12-3159
8 august	orchestra	78: hmv DB 21570
1950		45: victor 49-3159
		45: hmv 7ER 5004/7R 170
		lp: victor LM 1176/LM 1877
		lp: rca AGM1-5280
		cd: rca/bmg GD 60922
		cd: archipel ARPCD 0056
london	new symphony	lp: victor LM 2593/LSC 2593/
19-20	luboff choir	LSC 5004/VCS 7007
july		lp: quintessence PMC 7019
1961		cd: rca/bmg GD 61296/GD 89297/
		09026 625992/09026 684432
new york	his symphony	lp: bach guild 70696
19-21	orchestra	lp: vanguard SRV 363/VSD 707
april	kipnis,	cd: vanguard OVC 4021/OVC 8009
1967	harpsichord	

jesus christus gottessohn/oster-oratorium

philadelphia	philadelphia	78: victor M 401
5 april	orchestra	cd: pearl GEMMCDS 9098
1937		
new york	new york	lp: new york philharmonic NYP 821-822
6 april	philharmonic	cd: theo van der burg (netherlands)
1947		
new york	his symphony	lp: victor LM 1176/LM 2042
8 august	orchestra	lp: rca AGM1-5280
1950		cd: rca/bmg GD 60922
		cd: archipel ARPCD 0056
new york	american	unpublished recording
13-18	symphony	
april		
1963		
prague	czech	lp: decca PFS 4278
7-8	philharmonic	lp: decca (germany) 642.297
september		lp: london (usa) SPC 21096
1972		lp: supraphon 1110 1953
		cd: decca 421 6292/448 9462/475 1452
		also unpublished video recording

bach/**komm süsser tod/schemellis gesangbuch**

camden nj 28 october 1933	philadelphia orchestra	78: victor M 236/M 243 78: hmv DB 2274 cd: pearl GEMMCDS 9098 cd: grammofono AB 78782 cd: history 20.3290 cd: allegro CDO 1011 cd: membran 222174
new york 8 july 1941	all-american symphony	78: columbia (usa) X 220 cd: cala CACD 0527
new york 25 july 1950	his symphony orchestra	78: victor 12-3087 45: victor 49-3087 lp: victor LM 1176/LRM 7033 lp: hmv BLP 1074 cd: rca/bmg GD 60922 cd: archipel ARPCD 0056
chicago 2 january 1958	chicago symphony	unpublished recording
new york 5-11 february 1958	his symphony orchestra	lp: capitol P 8489/SP 8489 lp: emi MFP 2062 lp: angel seraphim 60235 cd: emi CDM 769 0722/566 3852/ 574 0492 *recording completed on 26 februaty 1958*
new york 8 may 1970	american symphony	unpublished recording
london 16-19 april 1974	london symphony	lp: rca ARL1-0880/AGL1-3656/ GL 42921/VL 42054 cd: rca/bmg 09026 612672/09026 626052/ 09026 684432

magnificat: unspecified excerpts

philadelphia 3-7 november 1967	philadelphia orchestra singing city choir	unpublished recording

bach/**matthäus-passion**

los angeles 29 august 1946	hollywood bowl symphony greater los angeles choir beach gifford j.sullivan williams wintner	cd: patrick kittel (germany)
new york 9 march 1963	american symphony schola cantorum sills petrak boucher wildemann	unpublished rehearsal recording *recording may be incomplete*

see also entries:: o haupt voll blut und wunden & wir setzen uns mit tränen nieder bach/**mein jesu was für seelenweh/schelemmis gesangbuch**

philadelphia 28 november 1936	philadelphia orchestra	78: victor M 401 78: hmv DB 3405 cd: pearl GEMMCDS 9098 cd: history 20.3290 cd: allegro CDO 1011 cd: membran 222174
new york 1 april 1941	all-american symphony	78: columbia (usa) 19004 cd: cala CACD 0527
new york 23 march 1950	his symphony orchestra	78: victor M 1512 45: victor ERB 52 lp: victor LM 1133/LM 1875 lp: hmv ALP 1387 cd: theo van der burg (netherlands)
new york 15-17 august 1957	his symphony orchestra	lp: capitol P 8415/SP 8415 lp: angel seraphim 6094 cd: emi CDM 769 0722/CDM 565 9122/ 566 3852/574 0492
chicago 2 january 1958	chicago symphony	unpublished recording
prague 7-8 september 1972	czech philharmonic	lp: decca PFS 4278 lp: decca (germany) 642.297 lp: london (usa) SPC 21096 lp: supeaphon 1110 1953 cd: decca 421 6392/448 9462/475 1452 *also unpublished video recording*

nun komm der heiden heiland, chorale prelude

camden nj 7 april 1934	philadelphia orchestra	78: victor M 243 78: hmv DB 2274 cd: pearl GEMMCDS 9098
new york 15-16 january 1949	new york philharmonic	lp: new york philharmonic NYP 821-822
chicago 2 january 1958	chicago symphony	unpublished recording
philadelphia 25 february 1960	philadelphia orchestra	lp: columbia (usa) ML 5713/MS 6313/ MGP 17/Y-33228 lp: cbs 30061 cd: sony MH2K 62345

bach/**o haupt voll blut und wunden/matthäus-passion**

camden nj june 1922	choir	unpublished victor recording
philadelphia 28 november 1936	philadelphia orchestra	78: victor M 401 78: hmv DB 3405 cd: pearl GEMMCDS 9098 cd: grammofono AB 78782 cd: history 20.3290 cd: membran 222174
croydon 21 april 1973	london symphony	unpublished recording

orchestral suite no 2

new york 12-14 september 1950	his symphony orchestra baker, flute	45: victor WDM 1569 lp: victor LM 1176 lp: hmv (france) FALP 281 *excerpts* 45: victor ERA 244/ERB 521 lp: victor LM 1875/LM 1877 lp: hmv ALP 1387 cd: theo van der burg (netherlands)
new york 16-20 may 1968	american symphony sollberger, flute	cd: theo van der burg (netherlands) *recording also made at rehearsal*

organ prelude and fugue in e minor

philadelphia 12 december 1937	philadelphia orchestra	78: victor M 698/M 963 cd: pearl GEMMCDS 9098

organ fugue in g minor "great"

camden nj 7 april 1934	philadelphia orchestra	78: victor 1728 cd: pearl GEMMCDS 9098

bach/**organ fugue in g minor "little"**

camden nj 17 march 1931	philadelphia orchestra	78: victor 7437 78: hmv DB 1952 cd: pearl GEMMCDS 9098
philadelphia 1936	philadelphia orchestrra	film soundtrack recording *the big broadcast of 1937*
new york 14 november 1940	all-american symphony	78: columbia (usa) M 451 cd: cala CACD 0527
new york 25 july 1950	his symphony orchestra	78: hmv DB 21570 45: victor WDM 1569/ERA 69 45: hmv 7ER 5004/7R 170 lp: victor LM 1176 lp: rca AGM1-5280 cd: rca/bmg GD 60922 cd: archipel ARPCD 0056
new york 5-11 february 1958	his symphony orchestra	lp: capitol P 8673/P 8489/ SP 8673/SP 8489 lp: emi MFP 2062 lp: angel seraphim 60235 cd: emi CDM 769 0722/566 3852/ 574 0492 *recording completed on 26 february 1958*
moscow 17 june 1958	ussr large radio symphony	cd: scora CD 009
new york 18 march 1963	american symphony	unpublished recording
new york 3 february 1968	american symphony	cd: japanese stokowski society LSCD 23-24
new york 4-7 march 1971	syracuse symphony	unpublished recording
london 11 january 1973	new philharmonia	unpublished recording
london 16-19 april 1974	london symphony	lp: rca ARL1-0880/AGL1-3656/ GL 42921/VL 42054 cd: rca/bmg 09026 612672/09026 626052/ 09026 684432
vence 21 july 1975	rouen chamber orchestra	cd: japanese stokowski society LSCD 23-24 *recording made at stokowski's final conducting appearance; recording also includes rebearsal extract*

bach/**passacaglia and fugue in c minor**

philadelphia 28 january 1929	philadelphia orchestra	78: victor M 59 78: hmv D 1702-1703 lp: victor VCM 7101/VIC 6060 lp: dell' arte DA 9001 cd: grammofono AB 78586 cd: phonographe PH 5025-5026 cd: allegro CDO 1011 cd: music and arts CD 1173 *recording completed on 1 may 1929*
philadelphia 16 november 1936	philadelphia orchestra	78: victor M 401 78: hmv DB 3252-3253 cd: pearl GEMMCDS 9098 cd: andante 2985
new york 4 july 1941	all-american symphony	78: columbia (usa) X 216 cd: cala CACD 0527
new york 27 february 1944	nbc symphony	unpublished recording
los angeles 19 august 1945	hollywood bowl symphony	unpublished recording
new york 4 december 1949	new york philharmonic	lp: japanese stokowski society JLSS 19 cd: theo van der burg (netherlands)
new york 15 march 1950	his symphony orchestra	78: victor M 1517 lp: victor LM 1133/LRM 7033 lp: hmv BLP 1074
rome 30 april 1955	rai roma orchestra	unpublished recording

bach/passacaglia and fugue in c minor/concluded

new york 5-11 february 1958	his symphony orchestra	lp: capitol P 8489/SP 8489 lp: emi MFP 2062 lp: angel seraphim 60235 cd: emi CDM 769 0722/566 3852/ 574 0492 *recording completed on 26 february 1958*
paris 12 may 1958	orchestre national	unpublished recording
london 30 july 1963	london symphony	unpublished recording
tanglewood 15 august 1965	boston symphony	cd: theo van der burg (netherlands)
chicago 24 march 1966	chicago symphony	lp: japanese stokowski society JLSS 20 cd: theo van der burg (netherlands)
new york 23 march 1969	american symphony	unpublished recording *recording apparently also made at rehearsal*
saarbrücken 18 july 1969	saarbrücken radio orchestra	cd: SR MAS 372 *recording apparently also made at rehearsal; also unpublished video recording of rehearsal and performance*
geneva 30 august 1969	international youth festival orchestra	lp: audio visual enterprises AVE 30696
new york 22 april 1972	american symphony	unpublished rehearsal recording
prague 7-8 september 1972	czech philharmonic	lp: decca PFS 4278 lp: decca (germany) 642.297 lp: london (usa) SPC 21096 lp: supraphon 1110 1953 cd: decca 421 6392/448 9462/475 1452 *also unpublished video recording*

bach/**prelude from violin sonata no 3**

new york 20 july 1941	all-american symphony	78: columbia (usa) 11983 cd: cala CACD 0527
los angeles 26 august 1945	hollywood bowl symphony	cd: enno riekena (germany)
new york 15-17 august 1957	his symphony orchestra	lp: capitol P 8415/P 8650/ SP 8415/SP 8650 cd: emi CDM 769 0722/CDM 565 9122/ 566 3852/574 0492
new york 4 may 1969	american symphony	unpublished rehearsal recording
london 16-19 april 1974	london symphony	lp: rca ARL1-0880/AGL1-3656/ GL 42921/VL 42054 cd: rca/bmg 09026 612672/09026 626052/ 09026 684432
vence 21 july 1975	rouen chamber orchestra	unpublished rehearsal recording

prelude in b minor/wohltemperiertes klavier book 1

philadelphia 2 may 1929	philadelphia orchestra	78: victor M 243 78: hmv DB 1996/DB 2275 lp: dell' arte DA 9001 cd: pearl GEMMCDS 9098
new york 15 march 1950	his symphony orchestra	lp: victor LM 2042 lp: rca AGM1-5280 cd: rca/bmg GD 60922
new york 22 april 1972	american symphony	unpublished rehearsal recording
vence 21 july 1975	rouen chamber orchestra	cd: japanese stokowski society LSCD 23-24 *this was a rehearsal performance*

bach/**prelude in e flat minor/wohltemperiertes klavier book 1**

philadelphia 12 october 1927	philadelphia orchestra	78: victor 6786 78: hmv D 1464/D 1938 lp: dell' arte DA 9001 cd: pearl GEMMCDS 9098 cd: grammofono AB 78782 cd: history 20.3290 cd: allegro CDO 1011 cd: membran 222174
new york 11 july 1941	all-american symphony	78: columbia (usa) X 541 cd: cala CACD 0527
new york 4 november 1941	nbc symphony	cd: enno riekena (germany)
los angeles 29 july 1945	hollywood bowl symphony	unpublished recording
philadelphia 14 october 1966	philadelphia orchestra	unpublished recording
new york 5 may 1968	american symphony	unpublished recording
new york 8 may 1970	american symphony	unpublished recording
new york 29 december 1971	american symphony	unpublished recording
new york 22 april 1972	american symphony	unpublished rehearsal recording
prague 7-8 september 1972	czech philharmonic	lp: decca PFS 4278 lp: decca (germany) 642.297 lp: london (usa) SPC 21096 lp: supraphon 1110 1953 cd: decca 421 6392/448 9462/475 1452 *also unpublished video recording*

bach/**sarabande from english suite no 3**

camden nj 7 april 1934	philadelphia orchestra	78: victor M 243 78: hmv DB 2275 cd: pearl GEMMCDS 9098 cd: grammofono AB 78782 cd: history 20.3290 cd: membran 222174 cd: cantus classics 500.150

sarabande from violin partita no 1

philadelphia 16 november 1936	philadelphia orchestra	78: victor M 401 cd: pearl GEMMCDS 9098 cd: grammofono AB 78782 cd: history 20.3290 cd: allegro CDO 1011 cd: membran 222174 cd: cantus classics 500.150
new york 5-11 february 1958	his symphony orchestra	lp: capitol P 8489/SP 8489 lp: emi MFP 2062 lp: angel seraphim 60235 cd: emi CDM 769 0722/566 3852/ 574 0492 *recording completed on 26 february 1958*

schafe können sicher weiden/cantata no 208

new york 8 august 1950	his symphony orchestra	78: victor 12-3159 45: victor 49-3159 45: hmv 7ER 5004/7R 170 lp: victor LM 1176/LM 1877 lp: rca AGM1-5280 cd: rca/bmg GD 60922 cd: archipel ARPCD 0056
rome 30 april 1955	rai roma orchestra	unpublished recording
london 19-20 july 1961	new symphony luboff choir	lp: victor LM 2593/LM 2800/LSC 2593/ LSC 2800/VCS 7007 lp: rca DPL1-0526 lp: quintessence PMC 7019 cd: rca/bmg GD 89297/09026 625992/ 09026 684432
new york 9 november 1964	american symphony	unpublished rehearsal recording
new york 19-21 april 1967	his symphony orchestra kipnis, harpsichord	lp: bach guild 70696 lp: vanguard SRV 363/VSD 707 cd: vanguard OVC 4021/OVC 8009

siciliano from violin and clavier sonata no 4

camden nj 28 october 1933	philadelphia orchestra	78: victor M 243 78: hmv DB 2275 cd: pearl GEMMCDS 9098 cd: grammofono AB 78782 cd: history 20.3290 cd: allegro CDO 1011 cd: membran 222174
new york 25 march 1950	his symphony orchestra	78: victor M 1512 45: victor ERA 244 lp: victor LM 1133/LM 1875 lp: hmv ALP 1387 cd: theo van der burg (netherlands)
new york 27 september 1953	cbs studio orchestra	cd: enno riekena (germany)
philadelphia 21 june 1965	philadelphia orchestra	unpublished recording
london 7 january 1974	london symphony	unpublished recording
vence 21 july 1975	rouen chamber orchestra	unpublished rehearsal recording

sinfonia/weihnachtsoratorium

philadelphia 30 april- 1 may 1929	philadelphia orchestra	78: victor 1742 78: hmv D 1741 cd: pearl GEMMCDS 9098
new york 5-11 february 1958	his symphony orchestra	lp: capitol P 8489/SP 8489 lp: emi MFP 2062 lp: angel seraphim 60235 cd: emi CDM 769 0722/566 3852/ 574 0492 *recording completed on 26 february 1958*
new york 19-21 april 1967	his symphony orchestra kipnis, harpsichord	lp: bach guild 70696
new york 29 december 1971	american symphony	unpublished recording

bach/**toccata and fugue in d minor**

philadelphia 6 april 1927	philadelphia orchestra	78: victor 6751 78: hmv D 1428 lp: victor VCM 7101 lp: neiman marcus (usa) lp: dell' arte DA 9001 cd: pearl GEMMCDS 9098 cd: magic talent MT 48002 cd: magic master MM 37022 cd: grammopfono AB 78586 cd: phonographe PH 5025-5026 cd: history 20.3290 cd: allegro CDO 1011 cd: andante 2985 cd: cantus classics 500.090 cd: documents 221708
camden nj 26 november 1934	philadelphia orchestra	78: victor 8697/M 1064 78: hmv DB 2572 cd: pearl GEMMCD 9488 cd: music and arts CD 1173
philadelphia 1937	stokowski, piano	film soundtrack recording *one hundred men and a girl*
philadelphia april 1939	philadelphia orchestra	*fantasia soundtrack recording* lp: top rank 30-003 lp: disneyland WDL 4101/ST 3926/STER 101 lp: buena vista BVS 101 cd: buena vista CD 020/60007 cd: pony canyon PCCD 00009 cd: avex AVCW 12048-12049/12163-12164 cd: pickwick DSTCD 452 vhs video: buena vista D 211322 vhs video: disneyland 101 dvd video: disney classics ZIDD 888113/888055
stockholm 25 may 1939	stockholm philharmonic	lp: orfeus (sweden) 1-73-1 cd: stockholm philharmonic CD 1 cd: theo van der burg (netherlands)
new york 4 july 1941	all-american symphony	78: columbia (usa) X 219 cd: cala CACD 0527
new york 12 december 1943	nbc symphony	unpublished recording
los angeles 15 july 1945	hollywood bowl symphony	unpublished recording

bach/toccata and fugue in d minor/continued

new york 22 march 1947	his symphony orchestra	78: victor 11-9653 45: victor 49-0263 45: hmv (france) 7RF 136 45: hmv (italy) 7RQ 134 lp: victor LM 2042/LRM 7033 lp: hmv BLP 1074 lp: rca AGM1-5280 cd: rca/bmg GD 60922 cd: archipel ARPCD 0056
rome 7 may 1953	santa cecilia orchestra	unpublished recording
london 7 march 1954	bbc symphony	unpublished video recording *bbc television*
new york 15 february 1957	his symphony orchestra	lp: capitol P 8399/P 8694/ SP 8399/SP 8694 lp: emi MFP 2145 lp: angel seraphim 60235 cd: emi CDM 565 6142/CDM 769 0722/ 566 3852/574 0492
chicago 3 january 1962	chicago symphony	vhs video: video artists international VAI 69603 dvd video: denon (japan) COBO 4061
baltimore 10 january 1963	baltimore symphony	unpublished recording
tokyo 13 july 1965	japan philharmonic	cd: platz (japan) P23G-535 cd: kapelle (japan) 32G 175807
budapest 2 february 1967	hungarian state orchestra	cd: theo van der burg (netherlands)

bach/toccata and fugue in d minor/concluded

monte carlo 26 july 1967	monte carlo philharmonic	unpublished recording
stockholm 9 august 1967	stockholm philharmonic	lp: bis BISLP 331 cd: theo van der burg (netherlands)
cleveland 13 may 1971	cleveland orchestra	unpublished recording
london 27-29 july 1972	london symphony	cd: rca/bmg 09026 684432 *unpublished rca/bmg lp recording, which also includes rehearsal extract*
prague 7-8 september 1972	czech philharmonic	lp: decca PFS 4278/D94 D2 lp: decca (germany) 642.297 lp: london (usa) SPC 21096 lp: supraphon 1110 1953 lp: pickwick IMPX 9033 cd: decca 417 8512/421 6392/433 8762/ 448 9462/467 8282/475 1452 *also unpublished video recording*

wachet auf ruft uns die stimme, chorale prelude

philadelphia 13 december 1963	philadelphia orchestra	lp: japanese stokowski society JLSS 03 cd: philadelpia orchestra POA 91 cd: theo van der burg (netherlands)
new york 9 november 1964	american symphony	unpublished rehearsal recording
new york 5 may 1968	american symphony	unpublished recording
london 16-19 april 1974	london symphony	lp: rca ARL1-0880/AGL1-3656/ GL 42921/VL 42054 cd: rca/bmg 09026 612672/09026 626052/ 09026 684432

bach/wir glauben all' an einen gott, chorale prelude

philadelphia 1 may 1929	philadelphia orchestra	78: victor M 59 78: hmv D 1710 78: electrola EJ 506 lp: dell' arte DA 9001 cd: pearl GEMMCDS 9098
new york 6 december 1942	nbc symphony	unpublished recording
new york february 1945	new york city symphony	unpublished recording
new york 20 february 1949	new york philharmonic	lp: new york philharmonic NYP 821-822 cd: theo van der burg (netherlands)
new york 25 july 1950	his symphony orchestra	45: victor WDM 1569 45: hmv 7ER 5004 lp: victor LM 1176 lp: rca AGM1-5280 cd: rca/bmg GD 60922 cd: archipel ARPCD 0056
chicago 2 january 1958	chicago symphony	unpublished recording
philadelphia 25 february 1960	philadelphia orchestra	lp: columbia (usa) ML 5713/MS 6313/ MGP 17/Y-33228 lp: cbs 30061 cd: sony MH2K 62345
new york 3-5 october 1963	american symphony	unpublished rehearsal recording
new york 21 november 1964	american symphony	unpublished rehearsal recording
prague 7-8 september 1972	czech philharmonic	lp: decca PFS 4278 lp: decca (germany) 642.297 lp: london (usa) SPC 21096 lp: supraphon 1110 1953 cd: decca 421 6392/448 9462/475 1452 *also unpublished video recording*

bach/**wir setzen uns mit tränen nieder/matthäus-passion**

new york 31 march 1942	nbc symphony collegiate choir	unpublished recording

ALFRED BACHELET (1864-1944)

chere nuit

los angeles 28 july 1946	hollywood bowl symphony connor	unpublished recording

MATTHIAS BAMERT (born 1942)

mantrajana

new york 11 december 1971	american symphony	unpublished rehearsal recording

SAMUEL BARBER (1910-1981)

violin concerto

new york 3-6 april 1964	american symphony laredo, violin	unpublished video recording *rehearsal performance also recorded*

adagio for strings

amsterdam 5 july 1951	concertgebouw orchestra	unpublished recording
new york 22-29 january 1957	his symphony orchestra	lp: capitol P 8385/P 8673/SP 8673 lp: angel 34481 lp: angel seraphim 6094 lp: emi SXLP 30174 cd: emi CDC 747 5212/CDM 565 6142
moscow 7 june 1958	ussr large radio symphony	cd: music and arts CD 787
new york 2-3 february 1968	american symphony	unpublished recording *also unpublished video recording of rehearsal*
new york 6 october 1969	american symphony	unpublished recording
new york 8 may 1970	american symphony	unpublished recording

barber/**mutations from bach**

new york 7 october 1968	american symphony	unpublished recording

die natali, chorale preludes for christmas

new york 18 december 1965	american symphony	unpublished recording

BELA BARTOK (1881-1945)

concerto for orchestra

houston 30-31 march 1960	houston symphony	lp: everest LPBR 6069/SDBR 3069 lp: world records CM 36/SCM 36 lp: hallmark SHM 590 lp: dell' arte DA 9013 cd: everest EVC 9008/EVC 9050 *EVC 9050 contains last movement only*
new york 9 november 1964	american symphony	unpublished rehearsal recording

music for strings, percussion and celesta

new york 18-20 december 1957	his symphony symphony	lp: capitol P 8507/SP 8507 lp: angel 34481 lp: world records CM 69/SCM 69 cd: emi CDC 747 5218 *recording completed on 21 january 1958*

miraculous mandarin, ballet suite

new york 18-19 may 1969	american symphony	cd: intaglio INCD 7421

dance suite

new york 26 october 1954	new york philharmonic	unpublished recording

two portraits for orchestra

new york 21 december 1963	american symphony	unpublished rehearsal recording

bartok/**rumanian folk dances**

new york 7-21 february 1954	cbs studio orchestra	cd: enno riekena (germany)

sonata for 2 pianos and percussion

new york 27 march 1952	yessin and viola, pianos jones and howard, percussion	lp: victor LM 1727 *recording completed on 3 april 1952*

GEORGE BASS

song of hope

new york 24 january 1964	american symphony	unpublished rehearsal recording

MARION BAUER (1887-1955)

sun splendour

new york 25 october 1947	new york philharmonic	unpublished recording

ARNOLD BAX (1882-1953)

tintagel, tone poem

london 7 march 1954	bbc symphony	unpublished video recording *bbc television*

LUDWIG VAN BEETHOVEN (1770-1827)

symphony no 2

chicago 7 october 1962	chicago symphony	lp: british stokowski society LS 4 cd: chicago symphony centenary CD 2
new york 21 october 1965	american symphony	unpublished rehearsal recording

symphony no 3 "eroica"

houston 17-18 october 1960	houston symphony	unpublished recording *recording may be incomplete*
new york 23 february 1963	american symphony	unpublished rehearsal recording
philadelphia 12-13 december 1963	philadelphia orchestra	lp: japanese srokowski society JLSS 03 cd: theo van der burg (netherlands) cd: ray osnato (usa)
new york 28 april 1968	american symphony	unpublished recording
new york 14-19 january 1971	american symphony	unpublished recording
london 10 february 1974	london symphony	unpublished recording
london 25-27 march 1974	london symphony	lp: rca ARL1-0600/AGL1-5247/GL 85247 cd: rca/bmg 09026 613402/09026 625142/ 09026 484432

symphony no 4

houston 3 december 1956	houston symphony	unpublished recording
new york 9-10 october 1966	american symphony	lp: japanese stokowski society JLSS 22 cd: theo van der burg (netherlands) cd: ray osnato (usa)

symphony no 5

camden nj 17 july 1931	philadelphia orchestra	victor L 7001 lp: british stokowski society LS 13 lp: japanese stokowski society JLSS 13 lp: neiman marcus (usa) cd: music and arts CD 1173 *L 7001 was an experimental 33.1/3 rpm recording (symphonic transcription disc)*
philadelphia 21-30 july 1931	philadelphia orchestra	cd: philadelphia orchestra POA 100 cd: theo van der burg (netherlands)
philadelphia november 1931	philadelphia orchestra	unpublished bell telephone recording *rehearsal performance of second movement only*
philadelphia 16 march 1932	philadelphia orchestra	unpublished bell telephone recording *rehearsal performance*
new york 14 november 1941	all-american symphony	78: columbia (usa) M 451 cd: american stokowski society LSSACD 4 cd: music and arts CD 857
new york 26 december 1943	nbc symphony	lp: japanese stokowski society JLSS 13 cd: enno riekeno (germany) cd: ray osnato (usa)
rome 8 may 1955	rai roma orchestra	unpublished recording
philadelphia 17 december 1962	philadelphia orchestra	unpublished recording
new york 24 april 1965	american symphony	unpublished rehearsal recording

beethoven/symphony no 5/concluded

tokyo 13 july 1965	japan philharmonic	cd: platz (japan) P23G-535 cd: kapelle (japan) 32G 175807
monte carlo 26 july 1967	monte carlo philharmonic	unpublished recording
new york 5 may 1968	american symphony	cd: memories HR 4495-4497
croydon 8 september 1969	london philharmonic	dvd video: emi classic archive DVA 492 8429
walthamstow 9-10 september 1969	london philharmonic	lp: decca PFS 4179/DPA 599-600 lp: london (usa) SPC 21042 cd: decca 430 2182/475 6090
syracuse 4-7 march 1971	syracuse symphony	unpublished rehearsal recording

beethoven/**symphony no 6 "pastoral"**

philadelphia april 1939	philadelphia orchestra	*fantasia soundtrack recording* lp: top rank 30-003 lp: disneyland WDL 4101/ST 3926/STER 101 lp: buena vista BVS 101 cd: buena vista CD 020/60007 cd: pony canyon PCCD 00009 cd: avex AVCW 12048-12049/12163-12164 vhs video: buena vista D 211322 vhs video: disneyland 101 dvd video: disney classics ZIDD 888113/888055
new york 24 march 1942	nbc symphony	unpublished recording
new york 20 february 1945	new york city symphony	78: victor M 1032 lp: rca camden CAL 198 cd: history 205.652303 cd: cala CACD 0523 cd: documents 221708
new york 30 october 1949	new york philharmonic	lp: japanese stokowski society JLSS 09
new york 18-19 march 1954	nbc symphony	lp: victor LM 1830 lp: hmv ALP 1268 lp: british stokowski society LS 10 cd: theo van der burg (netherlands) cd: cala awaiting publication *excerpts* lp: victor LM 1875 lp: hmv ALP 1387 cd: theo van der burg (netherlands) *rehearsal extracts* cd: rca/bmg 09026 684432 *complete editions contained stokowski's spoken introduction to the symphony*
houston 14-15 march 1960	houston symphony	unpublished recording *recording may be incomplete*
new york 23 january 1966	american symphony	cd: ray osnato (usa)

beethoven/**symphony no 7**

philadelphia 6 april 1927	philadelphia orchestra	78: victor M 17 78: hmv D 1639-1643/D 7676-7680 78: electrola EJ 444-448 lp: rca camden CAL 212 lp: parnassus 5 lp: neiman marcus (usa) lp: british stokowski society LS 13 cd: biddulph WHL 033 cd: history 205.652303 *recording completed on 15 and 25 april 1927; original victor issue and biddulph re-issue contain stokowski's spoken outline of themes*
new york 22 november 1942	nbc symphony	unpublished recording
los angeles 30 july 1946	hollywood bowl symphony	unpublished recording
illinois 12 november 1952	university of illinois symphony	unpublished recording
houston 20-21 october 1958	houston symphony	unpublished recording
new york 17 december 1958	symphony of the air	lp: united artists UAS 7003/UAS 8003 lp: quintessence PMC 7110 cd: rediscovery RD 009
london 23 july 1963	bbc symphony	cd: bbc legends BBCL 40052
new york 3-5 october 1963	american symphony	unpublished rehearsal recording
philadelphia 14 october 1966	philadelphia orchestra	unpublished recording

beethoven/symphony no 7/concluded

budapest 2 february 1967	hungarian state orchestra	cd: theo van der burg (netherlands)
boston 13 january 1968	boston symphony	cd: memories HR 4495-4497 cd: ray osnato (usa)
new york 4 may 1969	american symphony	unpublished recording
st moritz 30 august 1969	international festival youth orchestra	unpublished video recording
cleveland 13 may 1971	cleveland orchestra	unpublished recording
london 11 january 1973	new philharmonia	unpublished recording
london 17-18 january 1973	new philharmonia	lp: decca PFS 4342 lp: london (usa) SPC 21139 cd: decca 430 2182/475 6090

symphony no 8

camden nj 20 may 1920	philadelphia orchestra	78: victor 74661/6243 78: hmv 3-0579/DB 385 lp: british stokowski society LS 3 *second movement only*
houston 27 march 1957	houston symphony	unpublished recording
chicago 24 march 1966	chicago symphony	lp: japanese stokowski society JLSS 20 cd: chicago symphony CSO 90-92 cd: ray osnato (usa)
london 10 february 1974	london symphony	unpublished recording

beethoven/**symphony no 9 "choral"**

camden nj 30 april 1934	philadelphia orchestrra and chorus davies cathcart betts lowenthal	78: victor M 236 78: hmv DB 2327-2335 cd: american stokowski society LSSACD 3 cd: music and arts CD 846 cd: grammofono AB 78577 cd: history 20.3290 cd: magic masters MM 37065 cd: magic talent MT 48081
new york 11 november 1941	nbc symphony westminster choir brown heidt horne whisonant	unpublished recording *only the final movement was actually broadcast*
los angeles 1945-1946	hollywood bowl symphony greater los angeles chorus unspecified soloists	78: international artists limited edition 1A 2328 *final movement only*
new york 12 april 1947	new york philharmonic westminster choir boerner merriman dame duncan	lp: japanese stokowski society JLSS 10 cd: theo van der burg (netherlands) *JLSS 10 contained final movement only;* *performance was dated by theo van der burg* *as 4 december 1949*
houston 27 march 1957	houston symphony houston chorale hinkle dinwoodey petrak froman	unpublished recording *final movement only*
new york 21-22 may 1967	american symphony westminster choir kusmin stanford kolk hayes	unpublished recording

beethoven/symphony no 9/concluded

london 20-21 september 1967	london symphony lso chorus harper watts young mcintyre	lp: decca PFS 4183/DPA 599-600/VIV 1 lp: decca (germany) 641.800 lp: london (usa) SPC 21043/STS 15538 cd: decca 421 6362/452 4872/475 6090
croydon 23 september 1967	london symphony lso chorus harper watts young mcintyre	cd: music and arts CD 943
new york 3 may 1970	american symphony westminster choir floyd bonazzi marek clatworthy	unpublished recording
new york 22-23 april 1972	american symphony yale glee club boatwright parker shadley hill	unpublished recording *rehearsal performance apparently also recorded*

piano concerto no 5 "emperor"

new york 1-4 march 1966	american symphony gould, piano	lp: columbia (usa) ML 6288/MS 6888/ MP 3888/Y4-34640 lp: cbs 72483 cd: sony SM3K 52632/SX17K 52562
new york 14 april 1970	american symphony serkin, piano	cd: theo van der burg (netherlands) *this was a rehearsal performance*
new york 25-26 march 1972	american symphony masselos, piano	unpublished recording *rehearsal performance apparently also recorded*

beethoven/**triple concerto**

new york 14-16 january 1971	american symphony beaux arts trio	unpublished recording

choral fantasy

new york 21 october 1964	london symphony lso chorus serkin, piano	unpublished recording *recorded at a memorial concert for pierre monteux*

coriolan, overture

new york 26 october 1969	american symphony	unpublished recording
london 10 february 1974	london symphony	unpublished recording
london 28 march 1974	london symphony	lp: rca ARL1-0600/AGL1-5247/ AGL1-3656/GL 85247 cd: rca/bmg 09026 613402/09026 625142/ 09026 684432

beethoven/egmont, overture

camden nj may 1919	philadelphia orchestra	victor unpublished
london 10 september 1965	new philharmonia	unpublished recording
montreux 11 september 1968	orchestre de la suisse romande	cd: theo van der burg (netherlands)
new york 27 october 1968	american symphony	unpublished recording
london 17 january 1973	new philharmonia	lp: decca PFS 4342/D94 D2/SPA 409 lp: london (usa) SPC 21139 cd: decca 452 4872/475 6090
london 7 june 1973	new philharmonia	cd: theo van der burg (netherlands) cd: bbc legends BBCL 41152

die geschöpfe des prometheus, overture

new york 21 november 1964	american symphony	unpublished rehearsal performance
new york 15-17 january 1971	american symphony	unpublished recording *rehearsal was apparently also recorded*

leonore no 3, overture

philadelphia 8 february 1963	philadelphia orchestra	unpublished recording
new york 3 february 1968	american symphony	unpublished recording
london 25 april 1973	london symphony	unpublished recording
west ham march 1976	national philharmonic	lp: pye nixa PCNHX 6 lp: dell' arte DA 9003 cd: pye nixa CDPCN 6 cd: emi CDM 764 1402

beethoven/**first movement from moonlight sonata**

los angeles 2 september 1945	hollywood bowl symphony	unpublished recording
new york 29 march 1947	his symphony orchestra	78: victor M 236 78: hmv DB 2335 cd: american stokowski society LSSACD 3 cd: music and arts CD 846

die himmel erzählen die ehre gottes

london 19-20 july 1961	new symphony luboff choir	lp: victor LM 2593/LSC 2593 lp: quintessence PMC 7019 cd: rca/bmg 09026 625992/09026 684432

turkish march/die ruinen von athen

new york 9 february 1955	nbc symphony	lp: victor LM 2042 lp: british stokowski society LS 18 lp: japanese stokowski society JLSS 17 cd: theo van der burg (netherlands) cd: cala CACD 0543 *orchestra described for this recording as nbc symphony*
new york 17 january 1964	american symphony	unpublished recording

three equali for 4 trombones

new york 22-23 march 1969	american symphony	unpublished recording *rehearsal was apparently also recorded*

PAUL BEN HAIM (1897-1974)
piano concerto

new york 9 november 1963	american symphony rigai, piano	unpublished rehearsal recording

from israel, suite

new york 20 february 1959	symphony of the air	lp: united artists UAL 7005/UAS 8005 cd: theo van der burg (netherlands)

ARTHUR BENJAMIN (1893-1960)
from san domingo

los angeles 21 july 1946	hollywood bowl symphony	cd: enno riekena (germany)

MAXIM BEREZOWSKY (1745-1777)
adagio from the concerto a 6

new york 27 september 1953	cbs studio orchestra	cd: enno riekena (germany)

THEODOR BERGER (1905-1992)
rondino giocoso

new york 19-26 february 1958	his symphony orchestra	lp: capitol P 8458/SP 8458 cd: emi CDM 565 9122

IRVING BERLIN (1888-1989)
god bless america

new york july 1940	all-american symphony	78: columbia (usa) 17204

HECTOR BERLIOZ (1803-1869)

symphonie fantastique

london 18 june 1968	new philharmonia	cd: bbc legends BBCL 40182
london 19-20 june 1968	new philharmonia	lp: decca PFS 4169/SDD 495 lp: lomdon (usa) SPC 21031/JL 41028 cd: decca 2894 308672/430 1372/ 448 9552/475 1452
new york 26-27 april 1970	american symphony	classical recordings archive of america *issued only on tape cassette*

le carnaval romain, overture

philadelphia 1-5 december 1931	philadelphia orchestra	lp: bell telephone laboratories BTL 790 cd: theo van der burg (netherlands) *also unpublished rehearsal extract*
scheveningen 5 july 1951	concertgebouw orchestra	cd: audiophile classics APL 101.558 cd: q-disc MCCL 97018
hamburg 7 july 1951	ndr orchestra	cd: tahra TAH 485-486 cd: enno riekena (germany)
west ham march 1976	national philharmonic	lp: pye nixa PCNHX 6 lp: dell' arte DA 9003 cd: pye nixa CDCPN 6 cd: emi CDM 764 1402

l'enfance du christ

new york 13 december 1970	american symphony st patricks choir rung riegel stilwell devlin	unpublished recording

shepherds' farewell/l'enfance du christ

new york 29 december 1971	american symphony st patricks choir	unpublished recording

berlioz/**danse des sylphes/la damnation de faust**

new york 15 february 1951	his symphony orchestra	lp: victor LM 9029/LM 151
new york 24 november 1969	american symphony	unpublished recording
croydon 20 june 1970	london symphony	unpublished recording
london 22-23 june 1970	london symphony	lp: decca PFS 4220 lp: london (usa) SPC 21059/SPC 21112 cd: decca 414 5002/417 7792/433 8762/ 448 9552/475 1452

marche hongroise/la damnation de faust

camden nj march 1923	philadelphia orchestra	victor unpublished
philadelphia 12 october 1927	philadelphia orchestra	78: victor 6823 78: hmv D 1807 lp: victor VCM 7101/VIC 6060 cd: biddulph WHL 011 cd: grammofono AB 78586 cd: magic talent MT 48015 cd: magic master MM 370122 cd: phonographe PH 5025-5026 cd: cantus classics 500.090
los angeles 12 august 1945	hollywood bowl symphony	cd: enno riekena (germany)
london 11 january 1973	new philharmonia	unpublished recording
west ham november 1975	national philharmonic	45: nimbus 45204 lp: pye nixa PCNHX 4 lp: vogue CV 25103 cd: pye nixa CDCPN 4

LEONARD BERNSTEIN (1918-1990)

symphony no 1 "jeremiah"

new york 3 april 1967	american symphony godoy	unpublished recording

symphony no 2 "age of anxiety"

new york 28 april 1968	american symphony entremont, piano	unpublished recording

GEORGES BIZET (1838-1875)

symphony in c

new york 20 march 1952	his symphony orchestra	lp: victor LM 1706/VIC 1008 lp: victor (france) 630331 lp: victor (italy) A12R 0089 lp: hmv ALP 1181 cd: theo van der burg (netherlands) cd: archipel ARPCD 0242
london 4 june 1977	national philharmonic	lp: cbs 34567/76673 cd: sony MBK 39498/MBK 44894/ SBK 48264 cd: virtuoso 3602 cd: bella musica 31.6007/BMF 966 *stokowski's final recording sessions; bella musica editions incorrectly dated 1950*

carmen

los angeles 11 july 1946	hollywood bowl symphony and chorus koshetz heidt vinay pease	lp: japanese stokowski society JLSS 11-12 cd: eklipse EKRCD 31 *excerpts* cd: bella voce BLV 107.235 *this was a concert version of the opera*

bizet/**carmen, act 1 prelude**

camden nj 8 may 1919	philadelphia orchestra	78: victor 64822/796

carmen, suite

camden nj 30 april 1923	philadelphia orchestra	78: victor 66263-66264/1017 78: hmv DA 612 *this recording comprised marche des contrabandiers and garde montante only*
philadelphia 30 april 1927	philadelphia orchestra	78: victor 6873-6874/1356 78: hmv D 1618, D 1816 and E 531 victor L 1000 lp: american stokowski society LSSA 3 cd: biddulph WHL 012 *excerpts* 78: electrola EW 66 *recording completed on 2 may 1927; L 1000 was an experimental 33.1/3 rpm recording (symphonic transcription disc)*
new york 23 february 1945	new york city symphony	78: victor M 1002 78: hmv DB 9505-9508 45: victor WDM 1002 lp: victor LM 1069 cd: pearl GEMMCD 9276 cd: history 20.3290 *recording completed on 2 march 1945*
west ham 23-27 august 1976	national philharmonic	lp: cbs 34503/76587/MY 37260 cd: sony MYK 37260/MBK 44808

bizet/l'arlésienne, suite no 1

philadelphia 3-4 may 1929	philadelphia orchestra	78: victor M 62 78: hmv D 1801-1803/D 7363-7365 78: hmv (france) W 1089-1091 cd: biddulph WHL 012 cd: andante 2985 *this recording also included pastorale from suite no 2*
los angeles 1 september 1946	hollywood bowl symphony	unpublished recording
new york 29 february 1952	his symphony orchestra	lp: victor LM 1706/VIC 1008 lp: hmv ALP 1181 cd: theo van der burg (netherlands) cd: archipel ARPCD 0242 *adagietto only* lp: victor LM 1875 lp: hmv ALP 1387
west ham 23-27 august 1976	national philharmonic	lp: cbs 34503/76587 cd: sony MYK 37260/MBK 44808

l'arlésienne, suite no 2

new york 5 march 1952	his symphony orchestra	lp: victor LM 1706/VIC 1008 lp: hmv ALP 1181 cd: theo van der burg (netherlands) cd: archipel ARPCD 0242
west ham 23-27 august 1976	national philharmonic	lp: cbs 34503/76587 cd: sony MYK 37260/MBK 44808

bizet/**minuetto/l'arlésienne**

camden nj may 1919	philadelphia orchestra	victor unpublished

pastorale/l'arlésienne

camden nj 27 january 1922	philadelphia orchestra	78: victor 1113
philadelphia 8 december 1935	philadelphia orchestra	unpublished recording

see also version of pastorale included with 1929 recording of suite no 1

farandole/l'arlésienne

camden nj 27 january 1922	philadelphia orchestra	78: victor 1113

BORIS BLACHER (1903-1975)
variations on a theme of paganini

baden-baden 6 june 1954	swf orchestra	unpublished recording
cologne 25 may 1955	wdr orchestra	unpublished recording

ERNEST BLOCH (1880-1959)

schelomo, hebrew rhapsody for cello and orchestra

philadelphia 27 march 1940	philadelphia orchestra feuermann, cello	78: victor M 698 78: hmv DB 5816-5818 lp: victor LCT 14 lp: rca camden CAL 254 lp: neiman marcus (usa) lp: virtuosi (usa) RO32 LGR-9265 cd: biddulph LAB 042 cd: history 205.652303 cd: symposium 1236 cd: membran 222174 *rca camden issue described performers as warwick symphony orchestra*
new york 30 january 1949	new york philharmonic rose, cello	unpublished recording
new york 20 february 1959	symphony of the air neikrug, cello	lp: united artists UAL 7005/UAS 8005/ USLP 0099 cd: emi CMS 565 4272
new york 3 december 1967	american symphony shapiro, cello	unpublished recording
new york 14 december 1969	american symphony gutman, cello	cd: theo van der burg (netherlands)

america, epic rhapsody

new york 2-3 february 1960	symphony of the air american concert choir	lp: vanguard SRV 346/VRS 1056/ VSD 2056/VSL 11020 cd: vanguard OVC 8014/08.801471

symphony for trombone and orchestra

houston 4 april 1956	houston symphony schuman, trombone	lp: japanese stokowski society JLSS 20-21 cd: theo van der burg (netherlands)

LUIGI BOCCHERINI (1743-1805)

minuetto/quintettino in e

camden nj 27 january 1922	philadelphia orchestra	78: victor 66058/798 78: hmv 2-947
philadelphia 4 may 1929	philadelphia orchestra	78: victor 7256 78: hmv D 1864/D 8110 lp: rca camden CAL 120 cd: music and arts CD 1173 *rca camden issue described performers as warwick symphony orchestra*
new york 1941	all-american symphony	columbia (usa) unpublished
los angeles 22 july 1945	hollywood bowl symphony	cd: enno riekena (germany)
new york 19-20 february 1958	his symphony orchestra	lp: capitol P 8458/P 8650/ SP 8458/SP 8650 lp: emi SXLP 30174 cd: emi CDM 565 9122 *recording completed on 4 may 1958*

ARRIGO BOITO (1842-1918)

prologo/mefistofele

los angeles 19 august 1945	hollywood bowl symphony and chorus moscona	unpublished recording
new york 16 october 1967	american symphony various choirs buckingham	unpublished recording

FRANZ CARL BORNSCHEIN (1879-1948)

the moon over taos

new york 9 october 1944	new york city symphony	unpublished recording

ALEXANDER BORODIN (1833-1887)

polovtsian dances/prince igor

camden nj october- december 1920	philadelphia orchestra	victor unpublished
camden nj april 1922	philadelphia orchestra	victor unpublished
camden nj 29 april 1925	philadelphia orchestra	78: victor 6514 cd: biddulph BID 83072
philadelphia 5 april 1937	philadelphia orchestra	78: victor M 499 78: hmv DB 3232-3233 lp: rca camden CAL 203 cd: dutton CDAX 8009 cd: biddulph WHL 027 cd: andante 2985 *rca camden issue described performers as warwick symphony orchestra*
los angeles 28 july 1946	hollywood bowl symphony	unpublished recording
new york 27 november 1949	new york philharmonic	unpublished recording
new york february 1950	his symphony orchestra and chorus	78: victor 10-4212 78: hmv DA 2073 45: victor 49-4212/WDM 1386 lp: victor LM 1054/LRM 7056/VIC 1043 lp: hmv (france) FALP 105 lp: hmv (italy) QALP 105 lp: rca camden CDEM 1071 cd: theo van der burg (netherlands)

borodin/polovtsian dances/prince igor/concluded

new york 18 december 1966	american symphony schola cantorum	unpublished recording
london 15 june 1969	royal philharmonic wno chorus alldis choir	cd: music and arts CD 847 cd: bbc legends BBCL 40692
london 16-17 june 1969	royal philharmonic wno chorus alldis choir	lp: decca PFS 4189 lp: london (usa) SPC 21041/SPC 21111 cd: pickwick IMPX 9033 cd: decca 417 7532/430 4102/433 6252/ 436 5062/443 8962/467 8282/ 475 6090
new york 14 december 1969	american symphony and chorus	unpublished recording

no sleep, no rest/prince igor

philadelphia 20 january 1962	philadelphia orchestra london	lp: melodram MEL 228 cd: di stefano GDS 2204 cd: bella voce BLV 107.235

in the steppes of central asia

new york 14 april 1953	his symphony orchestra	lp: victor LM 1816/LRM 7056 lp: victor (france) 630215 lp: quintessence PMC 7026 cd: theo van der burg (netherlands)

nocturne from the string quartet

new york 15-17 august 1957	his symphony orchestra	lp: capitol P 8415/P 8650/ SP 8415/SP 8650 lp: emi SXLP 30174 cd: emi CDM 565 9122

JOHANNES BRAHMS (1833-1897)

symphony no 1

philadelphia 25-27 april 1927	philadelphia orchestra	78: victor M 15 78: hmv D 1499-1503/D 7671-7675 victor LM 15 lp: cameo classics GOCLP 9009 cd: biddulph WHL 017-018 cd: arkadia 78548 *LM 15 was an experimental 33.1/3 rpm issue (symphonic transcription disc); original and most later issues contain stokowski's spoken outline of themes*
philadelphia 19 december 1931	philadelphia orchestra	bell telephone unpublished
camden nj 15 january 1936	philadelphia orchestra	78: victor M 301 78: hmv DB 2874-2878 lp: rca camden CAL 105 cd: andante 1973 *CAL 105 described performers as warwick symphony orchestra*
stockholm 25 march 1939	stockholm philharmonic	cd: bis BISCD 421-424 *rehearsal recording of second movement only*
new york 8 july 1941	all-american symphony	cd: american stokowski society LSSACD 4 cd: music and arts CD 857
los angeles 1 august 1945	hollywood bowl symphony	78: victor M 1402/DV 4 45: victor WDM 1402 lp: victor LM 1070 cd: dutton CDBP 9705 cd: cala CACD 0520 *DV 4 was a set of red seal deluxe vinyl discs*
los angeles 2 september 1945	hollywood bowl symphony	unpublished recording *final movement only was performed at this concert*

brahms/symphony no 1/concluded

rome 7 july 1953	santa cecilia orchestra	unpublished recording
paris 12 may 1958	orchestre national	unpublished recording
philadelphia 23 february 1960	philadelphia orchestra	unpublished recording
baltimore 21 february 1962	baltimore symphony	unpublished recording
philadelphia 8 february 1963	philadelphia orchestra	unpublished recording
new york 18 april 1964	american symphony	unpublished rehearsal recording
new york 20 november 1966	american symphony	unpublished recording
new york 7 october 1968	american symphony	unpublished recording
london 14 june 1972	london symphony	cd: intaglio INCD 7221 *also unpublished video recording*
london 15 june 1972	london symphony	lp: decca PFS 4305/OPFS 3-4 lp: london (usa) SPC 21090-21091/ SPC 21131 cd: decca 475 6090 cd: cala CACD 0524

brahms/**symphony no 2**

philadelphia 29-30 april 1929	philadelphia orchestra	78: victor M 82 78: hmv D 1877-1882/D 7686-7691 lp: british stokowski society LS 11 cd: biddulph WHL 017-018 cd: arkadia 78549 cd: archipel ARPCD 0059
new york 2 april 1950	new york philharmonic	cd: enno riekena (germany)
amsterdam 5 july 1951	concertgebouw orchestra	cd: q-disc MCCL 97018 cd: theo van der burg (netherlands)
munich 16 july 1951	bavarian radio symphony	cd: tahra TAH 485-486
bergen 8-9 june 1953	bergen symphony	unpublished recording
san francisco december 1953	san francisco symphony	cd: archive documents ADCD 200-201 *rehearsal extract*
chicago 2 january 1958	chicago symphony	unpublished recording
houston 10 november 1959	houston symphony	unpublished recording
new york 1 december 1962	american symphony	unpublished rehearsal recording
new york 16 october 1967	american symphony	unpublished recording
london 4-9 april 1977	national philharmonic	lp: cbs 35129/76667 cd: cala CACD 0531

brahms/**symphony no 3**

camden nj february 1921	philadelphia orchestra	victor unpublished *third movement only*
camden nj 18 april 1921	philadelphia orchestra	78: victor 74722/6242 *third movement only*
camden nj may 1921	philadelphia orchestra	victor unpublished *third movement only*
philadelphia 25-26 september 1928	philadelphia orchestra	78: victor M 42 78: hmv D 1769-1773 lp: rca camden CAL 164 lp: british stokowski society LS 1 cd: biddulph WHL 017-018 cd: arkadia 78548 cd: history 205.652303 *CAL 164 described performers as warwick symphony orchestra*
new york 4 november 1941	nbc symphony	cd: enno riekena (germany)
new york 27 february 1944	nbc symphony	unpublished recording
los angeles 16 july 1946	hollywood bowl symphony	unpublished recording
houston 18 march 1959	houston symphony	lp: everest LPBR 6030/SDBR 3030/ SRN 135/SQN 139 lp: world records T 102/ST 102 lp: hallmark SHM 551 lp: quadrifoglio VDS 319 cd: bescol CD 517 cd: everest OVC 9016

brahms/**symphony no 4**

camden nj 3 april 1931	philadelphia orchestra	78: victor M 108 lp: neiman marcus (usa) *M 108 published only in south america*
camden nj 4 march 1933	philadelphia orchestra	78: victor M 185 victor LM 185 cd: biddulph WHL 017-018 cd: history 205.652303 cd: archipel ARPCD 0059 cd: music and arts CD 1173 *recording completed on 29 april 1933; LM 185 was an experimental 33.1/3 rpm issue (symphonic transcription disc)*
new york 1 april 1941	all-american symphony	78: columbia (usa) M 452 lp: american stokowski society LSSA 4 cd: music and arts CD 845
new york 18 november 1941	nbc symphony	cd: enno riekena (germany)
new york 13-18 april 1963	american symphony	unpublished recording *rehearsal was apparently also recorded*
new york 1 october 1965	american symphony	unpublished rehearsal recording
new york 10-12 october 1971	american symphony	unpublished recording *rehearsal was apparently also recorded*
london 14 may 1974	new philharmonia	cd: bbc radio classics BBCRD 9107 cd: nippon crown (japan) CRCB 6017
walthamstow 17-20 june 1974	new philharmonia	lp: rca ARL1-0719 cd: rca/bmg 09026 625142/ 09026 684432

brahms/**piano concerto no 1**

new york 26 october 1969	american symphony ogdon, piano	cd: american stokowski society LSSACD 2 cd: music and arts CD 844 *both issues also include rehearsal extracts*

violin concerto

new york 25-26 february 1967	american symphony silverstein, violin	unpublished recording *rehearsal was apparently also recorded*

double concerto

new york 11 december 1971	american symphony r.ricci, violin g.ricci, cello	unpublished rehearsal recording

ein deutsches requiem

houston 4-5 april 1960	houston symphony houston chorale and concert choir endich d.ligeti	unpublished recording

alto rhapsody

houston 21-22 march 1960	houston symphony bible	unpublished recording

schicksalslied

london 4 november 1973	london philharmonic orchestra and chorus	unpublished recording

serenade no 1

new york 17 november 1960	symphony of the air	unpublished recording
new york july 1961	symphony of the air	lp: decca (usa) gold label CDM 3205 lp: varese DL 710031/DL 10031/ VC 81050 cd: mca classics MCAD2-9826

brahms/**menuetto/serenade no 1**

camden nj 12 november 1934	philadelphia orchestra	78: victor 1720 78: hmv DA 1462 cd: biddulph WHL 047
los angeles 5 august 1945	hollywood bowl symphony	unpublished recording

haydn variations

chicago 3 january 1962	chicago symphony	vhs video: video artists international VAI 69603 dvd video: denon (japan) COBO 4061
chicago 14 january 1962	chicago symphony	lp: british stokowski sociery LS 4
london 4 november 1973	london philharmonic	unpublished recording

academic festival overture

los angeles 16 july 1946	hollywood bowl symphony	unpublished recording
london 4 november 1973	london philharmonic orchestra and chorus	unpublished recording
london 21 june 1974	new philharmonia	lp: rca ARL1-0719 cd: rca/bmg 09026 625142/09026 684432/ 74321 709312/74321 845882

tragic overture

london 9 april 1977	national philharmonic	lp: cbs 35129/76667 cd: sony SBK 63287/575 4812

brahms/**hungarian dance no 1**

camden nj 21 may 1920	philadelphia orchestra	78: victor 1113
camden nj november 1922	philadelphia orchestra	victor unpublished
camden nj may 1923	philadelphia orchestra	victor unpublished
camden nj 17 march 1934	philadelphia orchestra	78: victor 1675 78: hmv DA 1398 45: rca camden CAE 192 lp: rca camden CAL 123 cd: music and arts CD 1173 *rca camden issues described performers as warwick symphony orchestra*
los angeles 11 august 1946	hollywood bowl symphony	unpublished recording
los angeles 23-30 august 1946	hollywood bowl symphony	78: victor 10-1302 45: victor 49-1293
west ham 19 november 1975	national philharmonic	lp: pye nixa PCNHX 4 cd: pye nixa CDCPN 4

hungarian dance no 5

camden nj 22 october 1917	philadelphia orchestra	78: victor 64752/797 lp: british stokowski society LS 3 cd: wing (japan) WCD 11 cd: philadelphia orchestra POA 100 *stokowski's first recording sessions*

hungarian dance no 6

camden nj 24 october 1917	philadelphia orchestra	78: victor 64753/797 lp: british stokowski society LS 3 *stokowski's first recording sessions*

HENRY BRANT (born 1913)

signs and alarms

new york 22 february 1953	cbs studio orchestra	cd: enno riekena (germany)

HAVERGAL BRIAN (1876-1972)

symphony no 28

london 7 june 1973	new philharmonia	lp: aries LP 1607 cd: theo van der burg (netherlands) *aries issue described performers as hamburg philharmonic orchestra conducted by albert*

BENJAMIN BRITTEN (1913-1976)

piano concerto

new york 27 november 1949	new york philharmonic abram, piano	unpublished recording

serenade for tenor horn and strings

new york 1 march 1972	american symphony riegel miranda, horn	unpublished recording

soirees musicales

los angeles 14 july 1946	hollywood bowl symphony	unpublished recording

variations and fugue on a theme of purcell/young person's guide

london 23 july 1963	bbc symphony	cd: music and arts CD 787 cd: bbc legends BBCL 40052

passacaglia from peter grimes

los angeles 14 july 1946	hollywood bowl symphony	cd: theo van der burg (netherlands)
houston 31 october- 1 november 1960	houston symphony	unpublished recording
new york 24 january 1964	american symphony	unpublished rehearsal recording

ALEXANDER BROTT (born 1915)

violin concerto

new york 16 october 1953	his symphony orchestra brunet, violin	cd: enno riekena (germany)

CHARLES BUTTERWORTH (1885-1916)

a shropshire lad, rhapsody

new york 13 february 1944	nbc symphony	cd: cala CACD 0528

WILLIAM BYRD (1543-1623)

pavane and gigue/fitzwilliam virginal book

philadelphia 19 april 1937	philadelphia orchestra	78: victor 1943 78: hmv DA 1637 lp: american stokowski society LSSA 5 cd: theo van der burg (netherlands) cd: music and arts CD 1173
philadelphia 21 june 1965	philadelphia orchestra	unpublished recording
london 15 june 1972	london symphony	lp: decca PFS 4351 lp: london (usa) SPC 21130 cd: decca 433 8762/448 9462/475 1452

CHARLES CADMAN (1881-1946)

spring dance of the willow wand; dance of sacrifice

los angeles 25 august 1946	hollywood bowl symphony	cd: enno riekena (germany)

THOMAS CANNING (1911-1989)

fantasy on a hymn tune by justin morgan

houston 30-31 march 1960	houston symphony	lp: everest LPBR 6070/SDBR 3070 lp: world records TP 79/PE 751 lp: vox STGBY 515040 lp: dell' arte DA 9013 cd: everest EVC 9004

JOSEPH CANTELOUBE (1879-1957)

chants d' auvergne nos 2, 3, 4, 5, 10, 12 and 13

new york 10-11 april 1964	american symphony moffo	lp: victor LSC 2795/LSB 4114/AGL1-4877 cd: rca/bmg 7831-2-RG/GD 87831/ 09026 626002/09026 684432

HENRY CAREY (1663-1743)

god save the queen/british national anthem

edinburgh 20 august 1961	london symphony edinburgh choral union	unpublished recording

JOHN CARPENTER (1876-1951)

carmel concerto

new york 20 november 1949	new york philharmonic	unpublished recording

ROBERT CASADESUS (1899-1972)

piano concerto no 2

new york 14 march 1948	new york philharmonic casadesus, piano	cd: cascavelle VEL 2012 cd: theo van der burg (netherlands)

PABLO CASALS (1876-1973)

o vos omnes

new york 8 may 1970	american symphony	unpublished recording

MARC ANTONIO CESTI (1618-1699)

tu mancavi a tormentarmi, crudelissima speranza

new york 6 february 1944	nbc symphony	unpublished recording
los angeles 4-5 august 1946	hollywood bowl symphony	unpublished recording
new york 28 february 1952	his symphony orchestra	45: victor WDM 1721 lp: victor LM 1721/LM 1875 lp: hmv ALP 1387 cd: theo van der burg (netherlands)
new york 25 october 1953	cbs studio orchestra	cd: enno riekena (germany)
new york 16-17 december 1958	symphony of the air	lp: united artists UAL 7001/UAS 8001 cd: emi CMS 565 4272

EMMANUEL CHABRIER (1841-1894)

marche joyeuse

new york 2 april 1950	new york philharmonic	cd: enno riekena (germany)

espana

camden nj 9 may 1919	philadelphia orchestra	78: victor 76421/6241 78: hmv DB 384
los angeles 5 august 1945	hollywood bowl symphony	unpublished recording
west ham november 1975	national philharmonic	45: nimbus 45204 lp: pye nixa PCNHX 4 lp: vogue CV 25013 cd: pye nixa CDCPN 4 cd: emi CDM 764 1402

ERNEST CHAUSSON (1855-1899)

poeme pour violon et orchestre

los angeles 29 july 1945	hollywood bowl symphony seidel, violin	cd: eklipse EKRCD 1401 cd: history 205.652303 cd: membran 222174

FREDERIC CHOPIN (1810-1849)

piano concerto no 2

new york 8 may 1970	american symphony zaremba, piano	unpublished recording

les sylphides, scenes from the ballet

new york 11 may 1950	his symphony orchestra	78: victor M 1394 78: hmv DB 21255 45: victor WDM 1394 lp: victor LM 1083/LRM 7022/VIC 1020 cd: theo van der burg (netherlands)

mazurka in b flat minor

philadelphia 12 december 1937	philadelphia orchestra	78: victor M 841 cd: biddulph WHL 027
west ham july 1976	national philharmonic	lp: cbs 34543/73589 cd: cala CACD 0529

chopin/**mazurka in a minor**

philadelphia 7 november 1937	philadelphia orchestra	78: victor 1855 78: hmv DA 1638 lp: peerless PC 33 cd: biddulph WHL 027
new york 16 october 1949	new york philharmonic	unpublished recording
houston 30-31 march 1960	houston symphony	lp: everest LPBR 6070/SDBR 3070/SDBR 3418 lp: world records TP 79 lp: vox STGBY 515040 lp: peerless PC 33 cd: everest EVC 9048 *peerless described performers as american symphony orchestra conducted by dean marshall*
philadelphia 6 february 1962	philadelphia orchestra	unpublished recording
new york 7 may 1972	american symphony	unpublished recording
london 13 june 1972	london symphony	lp: decca PFS 4351 lp: london (usa) SPC 21130 cd: decca 433 8762/448 9462/475 1452 cd: cala CACD 0525

prelude in d minor

philadelphia 7 november 1937	philadelphia orchestra	78: victor 1998 cd: biddulph WHL 027 *hmv allocated catalogue number DA 1639 but the disc was not published*
new york 8 november 1950	his symphony orchestra	lp: victor LM 1238
houston 30-31 march 1960	houston symphony	lp: everest LPBR 6070/SDBR 3070/SDBR 3418 lp: world records TP 79 lp: vox STGBY 515040 cd: everest EVC 9048
west ham july 1976	national philharmonic	lp: cbs 34543/73589 cd: cala CACD 0529

chopin/**prelude in e minor**

camden nj april 1922	philadelphia orchestra	victor unpublished
camden nj 6 november 1922	philadelphia orchestra	78: victor 1111
new york 8 november 1950	his symphony orchestra	lp: victor LM 1238

waltz in c sharp minor

new york 10 february 1955	nbc symphony	victor unpublished
houston 30-31 march 1960	houston symphony	lp: everest LPBR 6070/SDBR 3070/SDBR 3418 lp: world records TP 79 lp: vox STGBY 515040 lp: peerless PC 33 cd: everest SDBR 9048 *peerless described performers as americana symphony orchestra conducted by dean marshall*

JEREMIAH CLARKE (1674-1707)

trumpet voluntary

camden nj december 1924	philadelphia orchestra	victor unpublished
los angeles 5 august 1945	hollywood bowl symphony	unpublished recording
los angeles 11 august 1946	hollywood bowl symphony	unpublished recording
los angeles 30 august 1946	hollywood bowl symphony	78: victor 11-9419 78: hmv DB 6737 lp: rca camden CAL 153 *CAL 153 described performers as star symphony orchestra*
philadelphia 17 december 1962	philadelphia orchestra	unpublished recording
london 15 june 1972	london symphony	lp: decca PFS 4351 lp: london (usa) SPC 21130 cd: pickwick IMPX 9033 cd: decca 433 8762/448 9642/475 1452

CARLTON COOLEY (born 1898)

promenade from the eastbourne sketches

new york 24 march 1942	nbc symphony	unpublished recording

AARON COPLAND (1900-1990)

short symphony

new york 9 january 1944	nbc symphony	unpublished recording

variations for orchestra

new york 10 october 1965	american symphony	unpublished rehearsal recording

prairie night and celebration dance/billy the kid

new york 3 november 1947	new york philharmonic	78: columbia (usa) X 729 lp: columbia (usa) ML 2167 cd: wing (japan) WCD 39 cd: theo van der burg (netherlands) cd: cala CACD 0533

the red pony, suite

new york 13 october 1949	new york philharmonic	unpublished recording

quiet city

los angeles 6 august 1946	hollywood bowl symphony	unpublished recording

music for a great city

new york 9-10 march 1969	american symphony	unpublished recording

ARCANGELO CORELLI (1653-1713)

concerto grosso in g minor "christmas concerto"

new york 5 december 1964	american symphony	unpublished rehearsal recording
new york 25-26 july 1967	his symphony orchestra kipnis, harpsichord	lp: bach guild 70696 lp: vanguard SRV 363 cd: vanguard OVC 8009/08.800971

HENRY COWELL (1897-1965)

tales of our countryside, for piano and orchestra

new york 5 july 1941	all-american symphony cowell, piano	78: columbia (usa) X 235 lp: american stokowski society LSSA 6 cd: theo van der burg (netherlands)

koto concerto no 1

philadelphia 28 december 1964	philadelphia orchestra eto, koto	unpublished recording
tokyo 13 july 1965	japan philharmonic eto, koto	unpublished recording

american piper

new york 23 january 1949	new york philharmonic	cd: theo van der burg (netherlands)

persian set

new york april 1957	chamber orchestra soloists	lp: composers' recordings CRI 114 cd: citadel CTD 88123
new york 3 december 1958	contemporary music society	unpublished recording

largo and allegro

new york 15-17 november 1970	american symphony	unpublished recording

cowell/**thanksgiving psalm**

new york 18 december 1966	american symphony schola cantorum	unpublished recording

hymn and fuguing tune no 2

new york 26 october 1952	his symphony orchestra	unpublished recording
new york 25 october 1953	cbs studio orchestra	cd: enno riekena (germany)

hymn and fuguing tune no 5

new york 26 october 1952	his symphony	unpublished recording

PAUL CRESTON (1906-1985)

saxophone concerto

los angeles 26 august 1945	hollywood bowl symphony abato, saxophone	cd: enno riekena (germany)

toccata for orchestra

new york 25 september 1958	his symphony orchestra	cd: cala CACD 0539

partita for orchestra

new york 21 february 1954	cbs studio orchestra	cd: enno riekena (germany)

scherzo/symphony no 1

new york 8 july 1941	all-american symphony	78: columbia (usa) 11713 lp: american stokowski society LSSA 6 cd: theo van der burg (netherlands)

chant of 1942

new york 26 december 1943	nbc symphony	cd: enno riekena (germany)

corinthians XIII

new york 3 april 1965	american symphony	unpublished rehearsal recording

lydian ode

new york 13-18 april 1963	american symphony	unpublished recording *recording apparently also made at rehearsal*

LUIGI DALLAPICCOLA (1904-1975)

il prigionero

new york september 1960	new york city opera orchestra mcknight cassilly treigle	lp: private edition MR 2009

WILLIAM DAWSON (1898-1990)

negro folk symphony

new york july 1963	american symphony	lp: decca gold label DL 710077/DL 10077 lp: brunswick AXA 4520/SXA 4520 lp: varese VC 81056 cd: mca classics MCAD 9826

CLAUDE DEBUSSY (1862-1918)

ibéria/images pour orchestre

paris 12 may 1958	orchestre national	cd: music and arts CD 778
paris 13-16 may 1958	orchestre national	lp: capitol P 8463/SP 8463 lp: angel seraphim 60102 lp: emi SXLP 30263 cd: emi CDC 747 4232/CDM 565 4222/ 567 3132
new york 19 november 1967	american symphony	unpublished recording

danse sacrée et danse profane

camden nj 4 april 1931	philadelphia orchestra phillips, harp	78: victor M 116 78: hmv DB 1642-1643 cd: biddulph WHL 013 cd: andante 4978

childrens' corner, suite

new york 2 march 1949	his symphony orchestra	78: victor M 1327 45: victor WDM 1327 lp: victor LM 9/LM 9023 lp: rca ANL1-2604 *recording completed on 30 march 1949*
new york 3 october 1958	stadium symphony	lp: everest LPBR 6108/SDBR 3108/ SDBR 3327 lp: world records T 173/ST 173 cd: everest EVC 9023

debussy/**la mer**

london 20 june 1970	london symphony	unpublished recording
london 22-23 june 1970	london symphony	lp: decca PFS 4220/SDD 455/414 5001 lp: london (usa) SPC 21059/SPC 21109 cd: decca 417 7792/455 1522/475 1452
new york 26 march 1972	american symphony	unpublished recording *rehearsal was apparently also recorded*

trois nocturnes

philadelphia 7 november and 12 december 1937 and 9 april 1939	philadelphia orchestra and chorus	78: victor M 630 78: hmv DB 3596/DA 1742/DB 3981-3982 lp: rca camden CAL 140 cd: biddulph WHL 013 cd: history 205.652303 cd: andante 4978 *CAL 140 described performers as warwick symphony orchestra*
new york 11 october 1950	his symphony orchestra shaw chorale	45: victor WDM 1560 45: hmv 7ER 5011 (fetes only) lp: victor LM 1154 lp: victor LM 6129 (nuages only) lp: british stokowski society LS 6 *recording completed on 10 november 1950*
london 27-28 june 1957	london symphony bbc chorus	lp: capitol P 8520/SP 8520 lp: capitol P 8673/SP 8673 (fetes only) lp: angel seraphim 60104 cd: emi CDC 747 4232/565 4222/567 3132
leipzig 1 june 1959	gewandhaus orchestra and chorus	cd: music and arts CD 280
new york 6 april 1964	american symphony brearley choir	unpublished video recording *rehearsal was apparently also recorded*
new york 16-18 november 1968	american symphony and chorus	unpublished recording

debussy/**nuages/trois nocturnes**

philadelphia 2 may 1929	philadelphia orchestra	78: victor M 116 78: hmv D 1614 lp: neiman marcus (usa) cd: music and arts CD 1173

fetes/trois nocturnes

camden nj april 1922	philadelphia orchestra	victor unpublished
philadelphia 11 october 1927	philadelphia orchestra	78: victor 1309 78: electrola E 507 lp: neiman marcus (usa) cd: music and arts CD 1173
philadelphia 18 december 1935	philadelphia orchestra	unpublished recording

clair de lune/suite bergamasque

philadelphia 5 april 1937	philadelphia orchestra	78: victor 1812 78: hmv DA 1634 v-disc 122A 45: rca camden CAE 188 lp: rca camden CAL 123 cd: music and arts CD 1173 *rca camden issues described performers as warwick symphony orchestra*
philadelphia 24 may 1939	philadelphia orchestra	*unpublished fantasia soundtrack recording* dvd video: disney classics ZIDD 888113/ ZIDD 888085
los angeles 31 october 1943	hollywood bowl canteen symphony	cd: theo van der burg (netherlands)
new york 24 may 1947	his symphony orchestra	78: victor 10-1534 45: victor 49-1009/ERA 47 45: hmv 7ER 5011 lp: victor LM 1154 lp: british stokowski society LS 6 cd: cala CACD 0529
new york 5-15 february 1957	his symphony orchestra	lp: capitol P 8399/P 8694/ SP 8399/SP 8694 lp: angel seraphim 6094 lp: emi SMFP 2145 cd: emi CDM 769 1162/CDM 565 6142/ 567 3132
west ham 12-16 july 1976	national philharmonic	lp: cbs 34543/73589 cd: cala CACD 0529

debussy/**prélude a l' apres-midi d'un faune**

camden nj november 1917	philadelphia orchestra	victor unpublished
camden nj november 1921	philadelphia orchestra	victor unpublished
camden nj 28 april 1924	philadelphia orchestra	78: victor 6481 78: hmv 4-0642/DB 840
philadelphia 10 march 1927	philadelphia orchestra	78: victor 6696 78: hmv D 1768 lp: victor VCM 7107 lp: neiman marcus (usa) cd: andante 4978
philadelphia 27 march 1940	philadelphia orchestra	cd: biddulph WHL 013 cd: andante 4978 *unpublished victor 78rpm recording*
philadelphia 8 december 1940	philadelphia orchestra	78: victor 17700 cd: music and arts CD 1173
new york 14 march 1943	nbc symphony	cd: cala CACD 0526
new york 9 january 1944	nbc symphony	unpublished recording
los angeles 15 july 1945	hollywood bowl symphony	unpublished recording
los angeles 20 august 1946	hollywood bowl symphony	unpublished recording
new york 4 october 1949	his symphony orchestra	78: victor 12-1119 78: hmv DB 21297 45: victor 49-0942 lp: victor LM 1154/LRM 7024 lp: british stokowski society LS 6

debussy/prélude a l' apres-midi d'un faune/concluded

amsterdam 5 july 1951	concertgebouw orchestra	cd: globe GLO 6905 cd: audiophile classics APL 101.558 cd: q-disc MCCL 97018
munich 16 july 1951	bavarian radio orchestra	unpublished recording *bayerischer rundfunk*
frankfurt 31 may 1955	hessischer rundfunk orchestra	unpublished recording *hessischer rundfunk*
new york 5-15 february 1957	his symphony orchestra	lp: capitol P 8399/P 8673/ SP 8399/SP 8673 lp: angel seraphim 6094 lp: emi SMFP 2145 cd: emi CDM 769 1162/CDM 565 6142/ 567 3132
philadelphia 23 february 1960	philadelphia orchestra	cd: philadelphia orchestra POA 91
new york 18 april 1966	american symphony	unpublished recording
new york 23-27 april 1971	american symphony	unpublished recording *rehearsal was apparently also recorded*
london 14 june 1972	london symphony	cd: emi 577 5802 dvd video: emi classic archive 492 8429
london 14-15 june 1972	london symphony	lp: decca OPFS 3-4/SDD 455/D94 D2/ DPA 601-602 lp: london (usa) SPC 21090-21091/ SPC 21109 cd: decca 417 7792/433 8762/455 1522/ 475 1452

debussy/**la cathédrale engloutie/préludes**

camden nj 30 april 1930	philadelphia orchestra	78: victor M 116 lp: neiman marcus (usa) cd: biddulph WHL 013 cd: history 205.652303
new york 13 february 1944	nbc symphony	cd: cala CACD 0526
new york 13 february 1949	new york philharmonic	unpublished recording
london 10 september 1965	new philharmonia	unpublished recording
london 11 september 1965	new philharmonia	lp: decca LK 4766/PFS 4095/SDD 455 lp: london (usa) PM 55004/SPC 21006 cd: decca 417 7792/436 5312/455 1522/ 475 1452/475 3132

soirée dans grenade/estampes

philadelphia 22 december 1940	philadelphia orchestra	lp: neiman marcus (usa) cd: biddulph WHL 013 *unpublished victor 78rpm recording*
new york 21 february 1943	nbc symphony	unpublished recording
los angeles 22 july 1945	hollywood bowl symphony	cd: enno riekena (germany)
los angeles 6 august 1946	hollywood bowl symphony	unpublished recording
houston 24-25 october 1960	houston symphony	unpublished recording
philadelphia 16 march 1962	philadelphia orchestra	cd: japanese stokowski society LSCD 23-2
west ham 12-16 july 1976	national philharmonic	lp: cbs 34543/73589 cd: cala CACD 0529

debussy/**épigraphes antiques**

new york 1 december 1962	american symphony	unpublished rehearsal recording

le martyre de saint sébastian, suite

new york 28 march 1943	nbc symphony	unpublished recording

LEO DELIBES (1836-1891)

sylvia, scenes from the ballet

new york 16 may 1950	his symphony orchestra	78: victor M 1394 45: victor WDM 1394 lp: victor LM 1083/LRY 8000/VIC 1020 lp: hmv ALP 1133 cd: kenwest (usa) CD 605 *excerpts* cd: theo van der burg (netherlands)

valse lente and pizzicato polka/sylvia

los angeles 4 august 1946	hollywood bowl symphony	unpublished recording

flower dance/naila

los angeles 22 july 1945	hollywood bowl symphony	cd: enno riekena (germany)

DAVID DIAMOND (born 1915)

the tempest, overture

new york 10 october 1966	american symphony	lp: japanese stokowski society JLSS 22 cd: theo van der burg (netherlands)
philadelphia 14 october 1966	philadelphia orchestra	unpublished recording

ROBERT EMMETT DOLAN (1908-1972)

waltz from lady in the dark

los angeles 12 august 1945	hollywood bowl symphony	cd: enno riekena (germany)
los angeles 23 august 1946	hollywood bowl symphony	78: victor 10-1302 45: victor 49-1293
los angeles 1 september 1946	hollywood bowl symphony	unpublished recording

GAETONO DONIZETTI (1797-1848)

mad scene/lucia di lammermoor

philadelphia 19 january 1963	philadelphia orchestra sutherland	cd: philadelphia orchestra POA 100 cd: bella voce BLV 107.235

ARCADY DUBENSKY (1890-1966)

the raven, melodrama for speaker and orchestra

camden nj 9-10 december 1932	philadelphia orchestra de loache, speaker	78: victor 2000-2001 victor L 1006 cd: japanese stokowski society LSCD 20 cd: cala CACD 0501 cd: andante 4978 *L 1006 was an experimental 33.1/3 rpm recording (symphonic transcription disc)*

PAUL DUKAS (1865-1935)

l' apprenti sorcier

philadelphia 7 november 1937	philadelphia orchestra	78: victor M 717 78: hmv DB 3533-3534/DB 6038-6039 lp: rca camden CAL 118 cd: biddulph WHL 011 cd: pearl GEMMCD 9488 cd: magic talent MT 48002 cd: history 20.3290 cd: documents 221708 *CAL 118 described performers as warwick symphony orchestra*
philadelphia 10 january 1938	philadelphia orchestra	*fantasia soundtrack recording* lp: top rank 30-003 lp: disneyland WDL 4101/ST 3926/STER 101 lp: buena vista BVS 101 cd: buena vista CD 020/60007 cd: pony canyon PCCD 00009 cd: avex AVCW 12048-12049/ AVCW 12163-12164 cd: pickwick DSTCD 452 vhs video: buena vista D 211332 vhs video: disneyland 101 dvd video: disney classics ZIDD 888055/ ZIDD 888113

dukas/**fanfare/la péri**

new york 12 february 1957	his symphony orchestra	lp: capitol P 8385/P 8673/SP 8673 lp: angel seraphim 6094 cd: emi CDM 565 6142/575 4812
new york 3-6 april 1964	american symphony	unpublished video recording *rehearsal was apparently also recorded*

HENRI DUPARC (1848-1933)

extase

new york 7-9 may 1972	american symphony	unpublished recording
london 13 june 1972	london symphony	lp: decca PFS 4351 lp: london (usa) SPC 21130 cd: decca 433 8762/448 8762/475 1452

ANTONIN DVORAK (1841-1904)

violin concerto

new york 24 october 1947	new york philharmonic milstein, vioilin	unpublished recording

rondo for cello and orchestra

los angeles 12 august 1945	hollywood bowl symphony reher, cello	cd: enno riekena (germany)

serenade for strings

london 16-19 august 1975	royal philharmonic	lp: desmar DSM 1011 lp: decca (germany) 642.631 cd: emi CDM 566 7602

slavonic dance no 10 in e minor

new york 26 march 1972	american symphony	unpublished recording *recording incomplete*
prague september 1972	czech philharmonic	lp: decca PFS 4333/PFS 4351 lp: london (usa) SPC 21117/SPC 21130 lp: pickwick IMPX 9033 cd: decca 433 8762/448 9552

dvorak/**symphony no 9 "from the new world"**

camden nj december 1917	philadelphia orchestra	victor unpublished *third movement only*
camden nj 21 may 1919	philadelphia orchestra	78: victor 74631/6236 *abridged version of second movement*
camden nj may 1921	philadelphia orchestra	victor unpublished *abridged version of second movement*
philadelphia 15 may 1925	philadelphia orchestra	78: victor 6565-6569 cd: biddulph BID 83072 *recording completed in october and december 1925*
philadelphia 5-8 october 1927	philadelphia orchestra	78: victor M 1 78: hmv D 1893-1897/D 7640-7644 lp: rca ARL2-0334/CRL2-0334 cd: biddulph WHL 027 *original and most re-issues also contain stokowski's spoken outline of themes*
camden nj 22 october 1934	philadelphia orchestra	78: victor M 273 78: hmv DB 2543-2547 lp: rca camden CAL 104/CDN 1008 lp: supraphon 1010 3351-1010 3352 cd: japanese stokowski society LSCD 25 cd: grammofono AB 78552 cd: history 20.3290 cd: sirio 530027 cd: cantus classics 500.150 cd: andante 2985 *CAL 104 described performers as warwick symphony orchestra*
new york 26 july 1940	all-american symphony	78: columbia (usa) M 416 cd: music and arts CD 841
los angeles 14 july 1946	hollywood bowl symphony	unpublished recording *second movement only*

dvorak/symphony no 9/concluded

new york 10-12 december 1947	his symphony orchestra	78: victor M 1248/V-25 45: victor WDM 1248 lp: victor LM 1013 lp: hmv (italy) QALP 104 *also issued on cd by victor in japan*
new york 7 may 1967	american symphony	unpublished recording *rehearsal was apparently also recorded*
london 7 june 1973	new philharmonia	cd: theo van der burg (netherlands)
walthamstow 2-4 july 1973	new philharmonia	lp: rca ARL2-0334/CRL2-0334 cd: rca/bmg 09026 626012/09026 684432

WERNER EGK (1901-1983)

french suite after rameau

baden baden 15 may 1955	swf orchestra	unpublished recording
new york 14 october 1956	symphony of the air	unpublished recording

HENRY EICHHEIM (1870-1942)

chinese rhapsody

camden nj may 1923	philadelphia orchestra	victor unpublished

bali/symphonic variations

camden nj 12 november 1934	philadelphia orchestra	78: victor 14141-14142 cd: japanese stokowski society LSCD 20 cd: cala CACD 0501

japanese nocturne/oriental impressions

camden nj may 1923	philadelphia	victor unpublished
philadelphia 30 april 1929	philadelphia orchestra	78: victor 7260 78: hmv D 1936 cd: japanese stokowski society LSCD 20 cd: cala CACD 0501 *recording completed on 1 may 1929*
philadelphia 6 february 1962	philadelphia orchestra	unpublished recording
new york 14 december 1969	american symphony	unpublished recording

HALIM EL DABH (born 1921)

tahmeel fantasy

new york 3 december 1958	contemporary music society	unpublished recording

EDWARD ELGAR (1857-1934)

enigma variations

los angeles 27 august 1946	hollywood bowl symphony	unpublished recording
new york 21 november 1964	american symphony	unpublished rehearsal recording
prague 7-8 september 1972	czech philharmonic	lp: decca PFS 4333/D94 D2 lp: london (usa) SPC 21136 cd: decca 433 8762/475 1452 cd: cala CACD 0524 *nimrod only* lp: decca PFS 4351 lp: london (usa) SPC 21112/SPC 21130 cd: pickwick IMPX 9033
london 11 january 1973	new philharmonia	unpublished recording

GEORGE ENESCU (1881-1955)

rumanian rhapsody no 1

new york 22 march 1947	his symphony orchestra	78: victor 12-0069 78: hmv DB 6828 45: victor 49-0127 lp: british stokowski society LS 17 cd: theo van der burg (netherlands)
new york 20 february 1949	new york philharmonic	unpublished recording *rehearsal was apparently also recorded*
new york 17 april 1953	his symphony orchestra	lp: victor LM 1878/LRM 7043 lp: victor (france) 630349 lp: quintessence PMC 7023 cd: theo van der burg (netherlands)
london 7 may 1954	bbc symphony	unpublished video recording *bbc television*
turin 6 may 1955	rai torino orchestra	unpublished recording
new york 17 february 1960	rca victor orchestra	lp: victor LM 2471/LSC 2471/VCS 7077 lp: rca RB 16259/SB 2130/AGL1-3880/ AGL1-5259 cd: rca/bmg 09026 615032/09026 626022/ 09026 684432/09026 709312
philadelphia 19 january 1963	philadelphia orchestra	cd: bella voce BLV 107.235
philadelphia 21 june 1965	philadelphia orchestra	unpublished recording
new york 7 may 1967	american symphony	unpublished recording *rehearsal was apparently also recorded*

rumanian rhapsody no 2

new york 1 october 1953	his symphony orchestra	lp: victor LM 1878/LRM 7043 lp: victor (france) 630349 lp: quintessence PMC 7023 cd: theo van der burg (netherlands)

MANUEL DE FALLA (1876-1946)

el amor brujo

los angeles 13 august 1946	hollywood bowl symphony merriman	unpublished recording
los angeles 14 august 1946	hollywood bowl symphony merriman	78: victor M 1089 78: hmv DB 21039-21041 45: victor WDM 1089 lp: victor LM 1054/VIC 1043 lp: rca camden CDM 1071 cd: pearl GEMMCD 9276 cd: dutton laboratories CDBP 9705
new york 21 march 1948	new york philharmonic	unpublished recording
amsterdam 5 july 1951	concertgebouw orchestra	cd: q-disc MCCL 97018
hamburg 7 july 1952	ndr orchestra	cd: enno riekena (germany) cd: tahra TAH 485-486
san francisco december 1953	san francisco symphony	unpublished rehearsal recording
turin 8 may 1955	rai torino orchestra dominguez	unpublished recording
philadelphia 12 february 1960	philadelphia orchestra verrett	lp: longanesi GCL 61 lp: japanese stokowski society JLSS 1-2 cd: theo van der burg (netherlands)
philadelphia 25 february 1960	philadelphia orchestra verrett	lp: columbia ML 5479/MS 6147/Y-32368 lp: cbs 61288 cd: sony MPK 46449/SBK 89291/ SB2K 64340 *stokowski's first stereophonic recording with the philadelphia orchestra*
new york 21 december 1963	american symphony	unpublished rehearsal recording
london 15 september 1964	bbc symphony lane	cd: music and arts CD 770 cd: bbc legends BBCL 40052

falla/**ritual fire dance/el amor brujo**

new york 5 july 1941	all-american symphony	78: columbia (usa) 11879

spanish dance/la vida breve

philadelphia 8 december 1928	philadelphia orchestra	78: victor M 46 78: hmv DB 1949 cd: pearl GEMMCD 9276 cd: biddulph WHL 047 cd: magic talent MT 48033 cd: cala CACD 0501 cd: cantus classics 500.090

noches en los jardines de espana

new york 13 november 1949	new york philharmonic kapell, piano	lp: new york philharmonic NYP 821-822 lp: discocorp MLG 71/OPUS 71 cd: japanese stokowski society LSCD 25 cd: music and arts CD 771

el sombrero de 3 picos, suite

los angeles 11 august 1946	hollywood bowl symphony	unpublished recording
san francisco december 1953	san francisco symphony	victor unpublished
new york 19 november 1967	american symphony	unpublished recording

HAROLD FARBERMAN (born 1929)

evolution, section one

new york 22-29 january 1957	his symphony orchestra	lp: capitol P 8385 cd: emi CDM 565 6142

GABRIEL FAURE (1845-1924)

sicilienne/pelléas et mélisande

philadelphia 21 june 1965	philadelphia orchestra	unpublished recording

OSCAR LORENZO FERNANDEZ (1897-1948)

batuque/reisado do pastoreio

new york 9 january 1944	nbc symphony	unpublished recording

GREGOR FITELBERG (1879-1953)

polish rhapsody

philadelphia 8 january 1932	philadelphia orchestra	bell telephone unpublished

CHRISTOPH FOERSTER (1693-1745)

air in the form of a sarabande

new york february 1954	cbs studio orchestra	cd: enno riekena (germany)

LUKAS FOSS (born 1922)

recordare for orchestra

scheveningen 27 june 1951	residentie orchestra	cd: theo van der burg (netherlands)

STEPHEN FOSTER (1826-1864)

oh susannah !

philadelphia 1 may 1928	philadelphia orchestra	cd: cala CACD 0502 cd: magic talent MT 48033 cd: magic master MM 37031 *unpublished victor 78rpm recording*

CESAR FRANCK (1822-1890)

symphony in d minor

camden nj april 1922	philadelphia orchestra	victor unpublished *second movement only*
philadelphia 3-4 october 1927	philadelphia orchestra	78: victor M 22 78: hmv D 1404-1408/D 7635-7639 LM 22 lp: american stokowski society LSSA 3 cd: music and arts CD 1173 *recording completed on 11 october 1927; original issue and cd re-issue contain stokowski's spoken outline of themes; LM 22 was an experimental 33.1/3 rpm recording (symphonic transription disc)*
philadelphia 19 december 1931	philadelphia orchestra	bell telephone unpublished
camden nj 30 december 1935	philadelphia orchestra	78: victor M 300 78: hmv DB 3226-3231 cd: biddulph WHL 011 cd: history 205.652303 cd: membran 222174
houston 12 march 1957	houston symphony	unpublished recording
amsterdam 20 august 1970	netherlands radio philharmonic	cd: music and arts CD 657 *third movement* cd: rca/bmg 74321 308892
hilversum 24-25 august 1970	netherlands radio philharmonic	lp: decca PFS 4218 lp: london (usa) SPC 21061 cd: cala CACD 0525 cd: decca 475 1452
new york 1 november 1970	american symphony	unpublished recording

andante/grande piece symphonique

philadelphia 19 april 1937	philadelphia orchestra	78: victor 14947 lp: american stokowski society LSSA 3 cd: biddulph WHL 011

panis angelicus

philadelphia 15 january 1936	philadelphia orchestra	78: victor M 300 78: hmv DB 3318 lp: american stokowski society LSSA 3 cd: biddulph WHL 011 cd: edizioni mercurio MU 198

GIROLAMO FRESCOBALDI (1583-1643)

gagliarda no 2/libro delle gagliardi

camden nj 22 october 1934	philadelphia orchestra	78: victor 1985/M 963 78: hmv DA 1606 lp: american stokowski society LSSA 5 cd: theo van der burg (netherlands) cd: music and arts CD 1173
los angeles 5 august 1945	hollywood bowl symphony	unpublished recording
new york 4 april 1952	his symphony orchestra	45: victor WDM 1721 lp: victor LM 1721/LM 1875 lp: hmv ALP 1387 cd: theo van der burg (netherlands)
new york 16 december 1958	symphony of the air	lp: united artists UAL 7001/UAS 8001/ UAS 8003 lp: quintessence PMC 7110 cd: emi CMS 565 4272/566 8642
philadelphia 6 february 1962	philadelphia orchestra	unpublished recording
new york 27 april 1970	american symphony	unpublished recording

ANIS FULEIHAN (1900-1970)

concerto for theremin and orchestra

new york 26 february 1945	new york city symphony rockmore, theremin	cd: symposium 1253

invocation to isis

new york 25 november 1958	symphony of the air	unpublished recording

GIOVANNI GABRIELI (1557-1612)

sonata pian e forte/sacrae symphoniae

new york 16 december 1958	symphony of the air	lp: united artists UAL 7001/UAS 8001 cd: emi CMS 565 4272/566 8642
london 30 june 1959	london symphony	unpublished recording
london 22 august 1961	london symphony	cd: bbc legends BBCL 40592
philadelphia 6 february 1962	philadelphia orchestra	unpublished recording

canzon quarti toni a 15

new york 6 march 1952	his symphony orchestra	45: victor WDM 1721 lp: victor LM 1721
philadelphia 4 february 1964	philadelphia orchestra	unpublished recording

in ecclesiis benedicte dominus

new york 6 march 1952	his symphony orchestra	45: victor WDM 1721 lp: victor LM 1721
new york 21-22 may 1967	american symphony westminster choir	unpublished recording

GEORGE GERSHWIN (1898-1937)

piano concerto

saarbrücken 1972	swf orchestra leimer, piano	unpublished video recording

porgy and bess, orchestral suite

new york 1 october 1965	american symphony	unpublished rehearsal recording

summertime/porgy and bess

los angeles 28 july 1946	hollywood bowl symphony connor	unpublished recording

walking the dog/shall we dance?

new york 9-10 march 1969	american symphony	unpublished recording

ALBERTO GINASTERA (1916-1983)

variaciones concertantes

new york 23 february 1963	american symphony	unpublished rehearsal recording

fausto criollo, overture

new york 3-4 may 1970	american symphony	unpublished recording

ollontoy

new york 16-18 november 1968	american symphony	unpublished recording *rehearsal was apparently also recorded*

UMBERTO GIORDANO (1867-1948)

un di all' azzurro spazio/andrea chenier

philadelphia 19 january 1963	philadelphia orchestra corelli	cd: philadelphia orchestra POA 100 cd: bella voce BLV 107.235

PEGGY GLANVILLE-HICKS (1912-1990)

letters from morocco, for piano and orchestra

new york 22 february 1953	his symphony orchestra w.hess, piano	cd: enno riekena (germany)

ALEXANDER GLAZUNOV (1865-1936)

violin concerto

london 14 june 1972	london symphony marcovici, violin	cd: intaglio INCD 7221 *also unpublished video recording from bbc tv*
london 15 june 1972	london symphony marcovici, violin	lp: decca OPFS 3-4 lp: london (usa) SPC 21090-21091 cd: decca 455 1572 *recording may include segment from 14 june concert*

danse orientale/scenes de ballet

philadelphia 2 may 1927	philadelphia orchestra	78: victor 1335 78: hmv E 521 78: hmv (france) P 802 78: hmv (italy) AV 10 78: hmv (spain) AA 165 78: electrola EW 56 cd: cala CACD 0521

REINHOLD GLIERE (1875-1956)

symphony no 3 "ilya mourometz"

philadelphia 27 march 1940	philadelphia orchestra	78: victor M 841 45: victor WCT 1106 lp: victor LCT 1106 cd: biddulph WHL 005 cd: andante 4978
los angeles 20 august 1946	hollywood bowl symphony	cd: theo van der burg (netherlands)
new york 23 october 1949	new york philharmonic	unpublished recording
new york 6 march 1957	houston symphony	lp: capitol P 8402/SP 8402 lp: angel seraphim 60089 cd: emi CDM 565 0742
chicago 9 january 1958	chicago symphony	unpublished recording
new york 19 november 1967	american symphony	unpublished recording
cleveland 13 may 1971	cleveland orchestra	unpublished recording

russian sailors' dance/the red poppy

camden nj 17 march 1934	philadelphia orchestra	78: victor 1675 78: hmv DA 1398 lp: victor VCM 7101/VIC 6068 cd: biddulph WHL 005 cd: magic talent MT 48015 cd: phonographe PH 5025-5026 cd: history 20.3290 cd: cantus classics 500.090 cd: andante 4978
new york 14 february 1953	his symphony orchestra	lp: victor LM 1816 lp: victor (france) 630.215 lp: quintessence PMC 7026 cd: theo van der burg (netherlands) cd: emi 575 4812

MIKHAIL GLINKA (1804-1857)

jota aragonesa

los angeles 14 july 1946	hollywood bowl symphony	unpublished recording

kamarinskaya

new york 16 january 1965	american symphony	unpublished rehearsal recording
london 15 june 1969	royal philharmonic	cd: music and arts CD 847 cd: bbc legends BBCL 40692

CHRISTOPH WILLIBALD GLUCK (1714-1787)

alceste, overture

philadelphia 21 november 1931	philadelphia orchestra	bell telephone unpublished
philadelphia 30 november 1931	philadelphia orchestra	bell telephone unpublished

reigen seliger geister/orfeo ed euridice

camden nj 8 november 1917	philadelphia orchestra	78: victor 74567/6238 lp: british stokowski society LS 3
new york 19-20 february 1958	his symphony orchestra	lp: capitol P 8458/P 8650/SP 8458/SP 8650 cd: emi CDM 565 9122 *recording completed on 4 may 1958*
london 19-20 february 1961	new symphony luboff choir	lp: victor LM 2593/LSC 2593 cd: rca/bmg 09026 625992/09026 684432
boston 12 march 1965	boston symphony	unpublished recording

gluck/**ballet suite**

comprises music from armide, iphigénie en aulide and orfeo ed euridice

los angeles 5 august 1945	hollywood bowl symphony	unpublished recording
new york 8-17 august 1957	his symphony orchestra	lp: capitol P 8415/P 8650/SP 8415/SP 88650 lp: angel seraphim 6094 cd: emi CDM 565 9122 cd: rheo van der burg (netherlands)

ROGER GOEB (1914-1997)

symphony no 3

new york 29 april 1952	his symphony orchestra	45: victor WDM 1727 lp: victor LM 1727 lp: composers' recordings CRI 120 cd: citadel CTD 88123

FRANCOIS JOSEPH GOSSEC (1734-1829)

la nativité

new york 17 december 1967	american symphony	unpublished recording

LOUIS MOREAU GOTTSCHALK (1829-1869)

symphony no 2 "a montevideo"

new york 6 october 1969	american symphony	unpublished recording

MORTON GOULD (1913-1996)

latin-american symphonette

new york 8 july 1941	all-american symphony	78: columbia (usa) 11713 lp: american stokowski society LSSA 6 *third movement only*
turin 6 may 1955	rai torino orchestra	unpublished recording
philadelphia 17 december 1962	philadelphia orchestra	unpublished recording *third movement only*

spirituals for orchestra

new york 15 november 1942	nbc symphony	unpublished recording

dance variations for two pianos and orchestra

san francisco 22 november 1953	san francisco symphony whittemore and lowe, pianos	lp: victor LM 1858

american salute

los angeles 19 august 1945	hollywood bowl symphony	unpublished recording
new york 21 june 1965	american symphony	unpublished recording *recording may be incomplete*

recording of the march with american symphony orchestra may also survive from 1966

new china march

new york 14 march 1943	nbc symphony	cd: cala CACD 0526

red cavalry march

new york 14 march 1943	nbc symphony	cd: cala CACD 0526

CHARLES GOUNOD (1818-1893)

valse/faust

camden nj october- december 1922	philadelphia orchestra	victor unpublished
camden nj 1 may 1923	philadelphia orchestra	78: victor 66161/944 78: hmv DA 562 lp: british stokowski society LS 3

vous qui faites l' endormie/faust

los angeles 19 august 1945	hollywood bowl symphony moscona	unpublished recording
philadelphia 20 january 1962	philadelphia orchestra london	lp: melodram MEL 228 cd: di stefano GDS 2204 cd: bella voce BLV 107.235 cd: philadelphia orchestra POA 100

PERCY GRAINGER (1882-1961)

country gardens

new york 31 may 1950	his symphony orchestra grainger, piano	lp: victor LM 1238/ARL1-3059/ RL 10168 cd: theo van der burg (netherlands) cd: cala CACD 0542

danish folksong suite

los angeles 21 july 1946	hollywood bowl symphony grainger, piano	cd: archive documents ADCD 2003 cd: enno riekena (germany) *both issues incorrectly dated 15 july 1945*

early one morning

new york 31 may 1950	his symphony orchestra grainger, piano	lp: victor LM 1238/ARL1-3059/ RL 10168 cd: theo van der burg (netherlands) cd: cala CACD 0542 *recording completed on 8 november 1950*

grainger/**handel in the strand**

new yotk 31 may 1950	his symphony orchestrra grainger, piano	45: hmv 7ER 5046 lp: victor LM 1238/ARL1-3059/RL 10168 cd: emi 575 4812 cd: theo van der burg (netherlands) cd: cala CACD 0542

in a nutshell, suite

los angeles 21 july 1946	hollywood bowl symphony grainger, piano	cd: archive documents ADCD 2003 cd: biddulph WHL 041 cd: enno riekena (germany) cd: music and arts CD 1002 *archive documents and enno riekena incorrectly dated july 1945*

irish tune from county derry

new york 8 november 1950	his symphony orchestra grainger, piano	45: hmv 7ER 5046 lp: victor LM 1238/ARL1-3059/RL 10168 cd: theo van der burg (netherlands) cd: cala CACD 0542 cd: rca/bmg 09026 681332/09026 636282

mock morris

new york 31 may 1950	his symphony orchestra grainger, piano	45: hmv 7ER 5046 lp: victor LM 1238/ARL1-3059/RL 10168 cd: theo van der burg (netherlands) cd: cala CACD 0542

molly on the shore

los angeles 15 july 1945	hollywood bowl symphony grainger, piano	cd: music and arts CD 1002
new york 31 may 1950	his symphony orchestra grainger, piano	45: hmv 7ER 5046 lp: victor LM 1238/ARL1-3059/RL 10168 cd: theo van der burg (netherlands) cd: cala CACD 0542

my robin is to the greenwood gone

new york 31 may 1950	his symphony orchestra grainger, piano	victor unpublished

shepherd's hey

new york 31 may 1950	his symphony orchestrra grainger, piano	lp: victor LM 1238/ARL1-3059/RL 10168 cd: theo van der burg (netherlands) cd: cala CACD 0542 cd: emi 575 4812

ENRIQUE GRANADOS (1867-1916)

intermezzo/goyescas

los angeles 22 july 1945	hollywood bowl symphony	cd: enno riekena (germany)
new york 11 december 1947	his symphony orchestra	78: victor 12-0470/18-0169 78: hmv DB 6915 45: victor 49-0882 lp: victor LM 9029/LM 151 lp: british stokowski society LS 17 cd: theo van der burg (netherlands) cd: cala CACD 0542

EDVARD GRIEG (1843-1907)

piano concerto

los angeles 15 july 1945	hollywood bowl symphony grainger, piano	lp: international piano archives IPA 508 cd: archive documents ADCD 2003 cd: biddulph WHL 041 cd: history 206.652303 cd: music and arts CD 1002

peer gynt, suite

los angeles 18 august 1946	hollywood bowl symphony	unpublished recording

anitra's dance/peer gynt

camden nj 8 november 1917	philadelphia orchestrrea	78: victor 64768/799 lp: british stokowski society LS 3

jeg elsker dig

new york 18 april 1963	american symphony melchior	lp: ed smith EJS 322 *performance of the song is encored*

CHARLES GRIFFES (1884-1920)

the white peacock/roman sketches

los angeles 21 july 1946	hollywood bowl symphony	cd: enno riekena (germany)
new york 17 november 1947	new york philharmonic	78: columbia (usa) 19012 lp: columbia (usa) ML 2167 cd: smithsonian RD 103-7 cd: cala CACD 0533

FRANZ GRUBER (1787-1863)

stille nacht heilige nacht

camden nj june 1922	chorus	victor unpublished *experimental recording: versions recorded with and without stokowski playing organ part*
new york 1944	westminster choir	unpublished video recording

CAMARGO GUARNIERI (1907-1993)

3 dances: dansa brasileira; dansa selvagem; flor de tremembé

new york 9 january 1944	nbc symphony	unpublished recording

GENE GUTCHE (born 1907)

genghis khan

new york 22-23 march 1969	american symphony	unpublished recording *rehearsal was apparently also recorded*

GEORGE FRIDERIC HANDEL (1685-1759)

amaryllis, suite

new york 18 october 1963	american symphony	unpublished rehearsal recording

tamburino/alcina

new york 19-26 february 1958	his symphony orchestra	lp: capitol P 8458/SP 8458 lp: emi SXLP 30174 cd: emi CDM 565 9122

handel/**concerto grosso op 6 no 10**

new york 1 march 1972	american symphony	unpublished recording

harpsichord concerto in b flat

new york 19 november 1949	new york philharmonic landowska, harpsichord	lp: international piano archive IPA 106-107 lp: discocorp BWS 720 lp: new york philharmonic NYP 821-822 cd: japanese stokowski society LSCD 25 cd: music and arts CD 821

oboe concerto in g

houston 3-4 november 1958	houston symphony weaver, oboe	cd: theo van der burg (netherlands)

overture in d minor/chandos anthem no 2

camden nj 16 december 1935	philadelphia orchestra	78: victor 1798 78: hmv D 1556 lp: american stokowski society LSSA 5 cd: theo van der burg (netherlands) cd: music and arts CD 1173
los angeles 27 august 1946	hollywood bowl symphony	unpublished recording
new york 6-11 october 1970	american symphony	unpublished recording

largo/serse

camden nj april 1934	philadelphia orchesrra	victor unpublished
london 19-20 july 1961	new symphony luboff choir	lp: victor LM 2593/LSC 2593/VCS 7077 lp: quintessence PMC 7019 cd: rca/bmg 09026 625992/09026 684432

handel/joy to the world

new york 29 december 1971	american symphony saint patrick's choir	unpublished recording

messiah, selection from the oratorio

london 20 september 1966	london symphony lso chorus armstrong procter bowen cameron	lp: decca LK 4840/PFS 4113/SPA 284 lp: london (usa) SPC 21014 cd: pickwick IMPX 9007 cd: decca 433 8742 cd: cala CACD 0538

hallelujah chorus/messiah

new york 29 december 1971	american symphony saint patrick's choir	unpublished recording

pastoral symphony/messiah

camden nj 29 april 1929	philadelphia orchestra	cd: cala CACD 0502 cd: cantus classics 500.090 cd: magic master MM 37031 *unpublished victor 78rpm recording*
camden nj 15 march 1930	philadelphia orchestra	78: victor 7316 78: hmv D 1938 78: hmv (italy) AW 219 lp: rca camden CAL 120 cd: music and arts CD 1173 *CAL 120 described performers as warwick symphony orchestra*
new york 19 december 1943	nbc symphony	unpublished recording
new york 27 march 1947	his symphony orchestra	78: victor 11-9837 45: victor 49-0974/ERA 119
new york 17 december 1967	american symphony	unpublished recording
new york 29 december 1971	american symphony	unpublished recording

handel/**dead march/saul**

new york 8 may 1970	american symphony	unpublished recording
new york 6 april 1971	american symphony	unpublished recording

music for the royal fireworks

new york 24 april 1961	rca victor symphony	lp: victor LM 2612/LSC 2612/VICS 1513/ AGL1-2704 lp: rca RB 6522/SB 6522/VL 42054 lp: camden classics CCV 5002 cd: rca/bmg VD 87817/09026 626052/ 09026 612 072/09026 684432

water music suite

camden nj 30 april 1934	philadelphia orchestra	78: victor 8550-8551 78: hmv DB 2528-2529 lp: american stokowski society LSSA 5 lp: japanese stokowski society JLSS 10 cd: theo van der burg (netherlands) cd: music and arts CD 1173
houston 19-20 october 1959	houston symphony	cd: theo van der burg (netherlands)
new york 5 march 1960	new york philharmonic	unpublished recording
new york 17 april 1961	rca victor symphony	lp: victor LM 2612/LSC 2612/VICS 1513/ VCS 7077/AGL1-2704 lp: rca RB 6522/SB 6522/VL 42054 lp: camden classics CCV 5002 cd: rca/bmg VD 87817/09026 625992/ 09026 684432
new york 24 november 1969	american symphony	unpublished recording

HOWARD HANSON (1896-1981)

symphony no 4 "requiem"

new york 2 january 1944	nbc symphony	unpublished recording

serenade for flute, harp and strings

new york 27 march 1949	new york philharmonic wummer, flute cella, harp	cd: new york philharmonic NYP 9904/NYP 9915 cd: theo van der burg (netherlands)

ROY HARRIS (1898-1979)

symphony no 7

saint louis 1955	saint louis symphony	cd: theo van der burg (netherlands)

dance tunes/symphony no 4

new york 1941	all-american symphony	columbia unpublished

folkdance for percussion and strings

new york 12 october 1941	new york philharmonic	unpublished recording

folk rhythms of today

new york 19 december 1944	nbc symphony	unpublished recording

LOU HARRISON (1917-2003)

canticle no 3

new york 22 february 1953	cbs studio orchestra	cd: enno riekena (germany)

suite for violin, piano and small orchestra

new york 29 october 1952	his symphony orchestra a.ajemian, violin m.ajemian, piano	lp: victor LM 1785 lp: composers' recordings CRI 114 cd: composers' recordings CRI 836

happy birthday leopold stokowski !

new york 18 april 1972	american symphony	unpublished recording

HERBERT HAUFRECHT

2 fantastic marches

new york 25 november 1941	nbc symphony	cd: enno riekena (germany)

KARL AMADEUS HARTMANN (1905-1963)

symphony no 2

cologne 25 may 1955	wdr orchestra	unpublished recording *westdeutscher rundfunk*

FRANZ JOSEF HAYDN (1732-1809)

symphony no 31 "horn signal"

new york 7 may 1966	american symphony	cd: theo van der burg (netherlands) *this was a rehearsal performance*

symphony no 45 "farewell"

philadelphia 17 december 1962	philadelphia orchestra	unpublished recording *recording probably incomplete*
new york 1 march 1972	american symphony	unpublished recording

symphony no 53 "l' impériale"

new york 20 february 1949	new york philharmonic	lp: japanese stokowski society JLSS 15 cd: theo van der burg (netherlands) *JLSS was incorrectly dated 5 march 1949; rehearsal was apparently also recorded*
new york 25 may 1949	his symphony orchestra	78: victor M 1352 lp: victor LM 1073 lp: british stokowski society LS 18 lp: japanese stokowski society JLSS 15 cd: theo van der burg (netherlands) cd: cala CACD 0532

symphony no 60 "il distratto"

new york 18-19 january 1970	american symphony	unpublished recording

haydn/**symphony no 101 "clock"**

new york 6 november 1949	new york philharmonic	unpublished recording

violin concerto no 1

new york 4 december 1949	new york philharmonic stern, violin	lp: japanese stokowski society JLSS 16 cd: theo van der burg (netherlands)

harpsichord concerto in d

new york 21-23 october 1966	american symphony puyana, harpsichord	unpublished recording *rehearsal was apparently also recorded*

sinfonia concertante

housron 24-25 october 1960	houston symphony	unpublished recording

andante cantabile/string quartet op 3 no 5

camden nj december 1924	philadelphia orchestra	victor unpublished
philadelphia 4 may 1929	philadelphia orchestra	78: victor 7256 78: hmv D 1864/D 1995 lp: rca camden CAL 120 cd: music and arts CD 1173 *lp described performers as warwick symphony orchestra; work was described on original issue as eighteenth century dance*
los angeles 19 august 1945	hollywood bowl symphony	cd: enno riekena (germany) *incorrectly dated 12 august 1945*
los angeles 30 august 1946	hollywood bowl symphony	78: victor 11-9419 78: hmv DB 6737
new york 14 october 1966	american symphony	unpublished recording
new york 13 february 1969	american symphony	unpublished recording
new york 23 march 1969	american symphony	unpublished recording
new york 14 january 1971	american symphony	unpublished rehearsal recording
west ham november 1975	national philharmonic	45: nimbus 45204 lp: pye nixa PCNHX 4 lp: vogue CV 25013 cd: pye nixa PCPCN 4

VICTOR HERBERT (1859-1924)

indian summer

los angeles 2 september 1945	hollywood bowl symphony	unpublished recording

BERNARD HERRMANN (1911-1975)

berceuse for the fallen

new york 1 november 1970	american symphony	cd: theo van der burg (netherlands)

the devil and daniel webster, suite

new york 13 february 1949	new york philharmonic	cd: new york philharmonic NYP 9904/ NYP 9915

PAUL HINDEMITH (1895-1963)

symphony in e flat

new york 28 february 1943	nbc symphony	unpublished recording
los angeles 6 august 1946	hollywood bowl symphony	unpublished recording
new york 5 january 1947	new york philharmonic	unpublished recording

kammermusik no 2 (piano concerto)

camden nj 17 december 1932	philadelphia orchestra norton, piano	cd: andante 4978 *unpublished victor 78rpm recording*

violin concerto

new york january 1945	new york city symphony gross, violin	lp: town hall S 32

nobilissima visione

new york 23 january 1944	nbc symphony	unpublished recording

GUSTAV HOLST (1874-1934)

the planets

new york 14 february 1943	nbc symphony	lp: japanese stokowski society JLSS 14 cd: cala CACD 0526
hollywood 2-3 september 1956	los angeles philharmonic	lp: capitol P 8389/SP 8389 lp: angel seraphim 60175 lp: emi MFP 2134/SMFP 2134 cd: emi CDM 565 4232/567 4692
new york 5 december 1964	american symphony	unpublished rehearsal recording

ARTHUR HONEGGER (1892-1955)

symphony no 3 "liturgique"

new york 21-23 october 1966	american symphony	unpublished recording *rehearsal was apparently also recorded*

pacific 231

los angeles 14 july 1946	hollywood bowl symphony	cd: theo van der burg (netherlands)

ALAN HOVHANESS (1911-2000)

symphony no 1 "exile"

new york 6 december 1942	nbc symphony	unpublished recording

symphony no 2 "mysterious mountain"

houston 31 october 1955	houston symphony	unpublished recording
new york 25 september 1958	his symphony orchestra	cd: cala CACD 0539
new york 20 november 1966	american symphony	unpublished recording

hovhaness/**symphony no 3**

new york 14 october 1956	symphony of the air	unpublished recording

concerto for orchestra

new york 27 september 1953	cbs studio orchestra	cd: enno riekena (germany)

prelude and quadruple fugue

boston 6 march 1964	boston symphony	unpublished recording
tanglewood 21 august 1964	boston symphony	cd: theo van der burg (netherlands)

alleluja and fugue for strings

new york 27 september 1953	cbs studio orchestra	unpublished recording

christmas ode/triptych

new york 29 december 1971	american symphony valente	unpublished recording

thirtieth ode of solomon

new york 26 october 1952	his symphony orchestra	unpublished recording

ad lyram for chorus and orchestra

houston 18 march 1953	houston symphony houston chorale	unpublished recording
houston 12 march 1957	houston symphony houston chorale	unpublished recording

meditation on zeami

new york october 1964	american symphony	unpublished rehearsal recording

praise the lord with psaltery

new york 21-23 december 1968	american symphony and chorus	unpublished recording *rehearsal was apparently also recorded*

ENGELBERT HUMPERDINCK (1854-1921)

hänsel und gretel, overture

new york 22 september 1949	his symphony orchestra	78: victor 12-1321 78: hmv DB 21256 45: victor 49-1376 45: hmv 7ER 5016 45: hmv (italy) 7RQ 271 lp: victor LM 2042 lp: japanese stokowski society JLSS 17 cd: theo van der burg (netherlands) cd: cala CACD 0532

abendsegen/hänsel und gretel

london 19-20 july 1961	london symphony luboff choir	lp: victor LM 2593/LSC 2593 lp: quintessence PMC 7019 cd: rca/bmg 09026 625992/09026 618672/ 09026 684432

CHARLES HUPFELD (1894-1951)

when yuba plays the rhumba on the tuba down in cuba

new york 12 march 1949	new york philharmonic bell, tuba	lp: new york philharmonic 821-822 cd: theo van der burg (netherlands)

JACQUES IBERT (1890-1962)

escales

new york 15 february 1951	his symphony orchestra	45: victor WDM 1628 lp: victor LM 151/LM 6129/LM 9029 lp: british stokowski society LS 17 cd: theo van der burg (netherlands) cd: cala CACD 0542
paris 12 may 1958	orchestre national	cd: music and arts CD 778
paris 13 may 1958	orchestre national	lp: capitol P 8463/SP 8463 lp: angel seraphim 60102 lp: emi SXLP 30263 cd: emi CDM 565 4222/575 4812
houston 3-4 november 1958	houston symphony	unpublished recording *second movement only*
new york 3 april 1967	american symphony	unpublished recording

ibert/**scherzo féerique**

turin 6 may 1955	rai torino orchestra	cd: theo van der burg (netherlands)

ILYASHENKO

dyptique mongole

philadelphia 12 march 1932	philadelphia orchestra	bell telephone unpublished

MIKHAIL IPPOLITOV-IVANOV (1859-1935)

in a mountain pass/caucasian sketches

camden nj april 1922	philadelphia orchestra	victor unpublished
philadelphia 8 february 1963	philadelphia orchestra	unpublished recording

in a village/caucasian sketches

philadelphia 14-15 may 1925	philadelphia orchestra	78: victor 6514 cd: biddulph WHL 005/BID 83072
new york 3 november 1947	new york philharmonic	78: columbia (usa) M 729 cd: cala CACD 0533

ippolitov-ivanov/**in a mosque/caucasian sketches**

camden nj 22 october 1934	philadelphia orchestra	78: victor 1692 cd: cala CACD 0521 *victor catalogue number subsequently used for 1939 remake*
philadelphia 1939	philadelphia orchestra	78: victor 1692
new york 27 march 1947	his symphony orchestra	78: victor 11-9857 45: victor 49-0974/ERA 119
new york 1 december 1962	american symphony	unpublished rehearsal performance
new york 18-23 december 1966	american symphony	unpublished recording
new york 14 december 1969	american symphony	unpublished recording
new york 29 december 1971	american symphony	unpublished recording

procession of the sardar/caucasian sketches

camden nj 29 april 1922	philadelphia orchestra	78: victor 66106/796
philadelphia 11 october 1927	philadelphia orchestra	78: victor 1335 78: hmv E 521 lp: victor VCM 7101/VIC 6060 lp: rca camden CAL 123 cd: biddulph WHL 005 cd: magic talent MT 48015 cd: phonographe PH 5025-5026 cd: cantus classics 500.090 cd: history 20.3290 *CAL 123 described performers as warwick symphony orchestra*
west ham november 1975	national philharmonic	45: nimbus 45204 lp: pye nixa PCNHX 4 lp: vogue CV 25013 cd: pye nixa CDCPN 4 cd: emi CDM 764 1402

JOSE ITURBI (1895-1980)

soliloquy

los angeles 30 july 1946	hollywood bowl symphony	unpublished recording

CHARLES IVES (1874-1954)

symphony no 4

new york 26 april 1965	american symphony schola cantorum	unpublished recording *rehearsal was apparently also recorded*
new york 29-30 april 1965	american symphony schola cantorum	lp: columbia (usa) ML 6175/MS 6775 lp: cbs 72403/77424 lp: franklin mint 19-20 cd: sony MPK 46726
new york 17 december 1967	american symphony schola cantorum	unpublished recording
new york 14-17 november 1970	american symphony schola cantorum	unpublished recording *rehearsal was apparently also recorded*

symphony no 5 "new england holidays"

new york 11 december 1971	american symphony	unpublished recording *rehearsal was apparently also recorded*

largo cantabile

new york 7-21 february 1954	cbs studio orchestra	cd: enno riekena (germany)

orchestral set no 2

london 18-20 june 1970	london symphony	cd: intaglio INCD 742 cd: music and arts CD 787
london 22-23 june 1970	london symphony	lp: decca PFS 4203 lp: london (usa) SPC 21060 cd: decca 433 0172/448 9562

ives/**the unanswered question**

new york 22 february 1953	cbs studio orchestra	cd: enno riekena (germany)
tokyi 8 july 1965	japan philharmonic	cd: music and arts CD 787

robert browning overture

new york 14 october 1956	symphony of the air	unpublished recording
new york 18 december 1966	american symphony	unpublished recording
new york december 1966	american symphony	lp: columbia (usa) ML 6415/MS 7015 lp: cbs 72646 cd: sony MPK 46726/SBK 89290/ SK 89851

washington's birthday

new york 21 february 1954	cbs studio orchestra	cd: enno riekena (germany)

4 songs for chorus and orchestra: an election; lincoln the great commoner; majority; they are there

new york october 1967	american symphony gregg smith singers ithaca college concert choir	lp: columbia (usa) M4-32504 cd: sony MPK 46726
new york 16 october 1967	american symphony gregg smith singers ithaca college concert choir	unpublished recording

WERNER JOSTEN (1885-1963)

concerto sacro I

new york 9 june 1965	american symphony del tredici, piano	lp: composer's recordings CRI 100 cd: composer's recordings CRI 597
new york 21-23 december 1968	american symphony del tredici, piano	unpublished recording *rehearsal was apparently also recorded*

concerto sacro II

new york 9 june 1965	american symphony del tredici, piano	lp: composer's recordings CRI 100 cd: composer's recordings CRI 597

canzona seria

new york march 1971	dunkel, flute krilov, oboe shifrin, clarinet scribner, bassoon	lp: composer's recordings CRI 267 cd: composer's recordings CRI 597

jungle, tone poem

new york march 1971	american symphony	lp: composer's recordings CRI 267 cd: composer's recordings CRI 597
new york 23 march 1971	american symphony	unpublished recording

DMITRI KABALEVSKY (1904-1987)

colas breugnon, overture

los angeles 14 july 1946	hollywood bowl symphony	unpublished recording
new york 12 january 1947	new york philharmonic	unpublished recording

ERNEST KANITZ (1894-1980)

3 fantasies for orchestra

los angeles 1 september 1946	hollywood bowl symphony	unpublished recording

ULYSSES KAY (1917-1995)

brief elegy

new york 1 march 1972	american symphony	unpublished recording

suite for strings

new york 28 october 1952	his symphony orchestra	unpublished recording

ROBERT KELLY (born 1916)

sunset reflections/adironack suite

new york 18 november 1941	nbc symphony	cd: enno riekena (germany) *includes spoken introduction by stokowski*
new york 27 november 1941	nbc symphony	cd: cala CACD 0502 *unpublished victor 78rpm recording*

FRANCIS SCOTT KEY (1779-1843)

the star spangled banner/us anthem

new york july 1940	all-american symphony	78: columbia (usa) 17204

ARAM KHACHATURIAN (1903-1978)

symphony no 2 "the bell"

new york 23 january 1949	new york philharmonic	unpublished recording
new york 18 december 1958	symphony of the air	lp: united artists UAL 7001/UAS 8001 cd: emi CMS 565 4273

symphony no 3

chicago 15-21 february 1968	chicago symphony sauer, organ	lp: victot LSC 3067 lp: rca SB 6804/GL 42923 cd: rca/bmg 09026 625162/09026 684432

flute concerto

new york 18-19 january 1970	american symphony rampal, flute	unpublished recording

khachaturian/**gayaneh, ballet suite**

new york 27 march 1949	new york philharmonic	unpublished recording

sabre dance/gayaneh

philadelphia 14 october 1966	philadelphia orchestra	unpublished recording

lezghinka/gayaneh

philadelphia 21 june 1965	philadelphia orchestra	unpublished recording

GEORGE KLEINSINGER (1914-1982)

tubby the tuba

new york february 1949	new york philharmonic	unpublished rehearsal recording

OTTO KLEMPERER (1885-1973)

merry waltz/das ziel

london 14 may 1974	new philharmonia	cd: bbc radio classics BBCRD 9107 cd: nippon crown (japan) CRCB 6017

ZOLTAN KODALY (1882-1967)

dances of galanta

los angeles 21 july 1946	hollywood bowl symphony	cd: enno riekena (germany)

hary janos, suite from the incidental music

houston 24-25 october 1960	houston symphony	unpublished recording
new york 9 november 1963	american symphony	unpublished rehearsal recording
budapest 3 february 1967	hungarian radio orchestra	lp: british stokowski society LS 2 cd: music and arts CD 771
new york 6 may 1967	american symphony	unpublished rehearsal recording *intermezzo movement only*

te deum

new york 9 may 1968	youth performers orchestra and chorus j.mathis myhal williams a.ord	lp: audio EC 68006 cd: music and arts CD 771

ERICH WOLFGANG KORNGOLD (1897-1957)

mariettas lied/die tote stadt

los angeles 28 july 1946	hollywood bowl symphony connor	unpublished recording

FRITZ KREISLER (1875-1962)

caprice viennois pour violon et orchestre

los angeles 14 july 1946	hollywood bowl symphony wicks, violin	lp: musenkranz GMV 13Y

ROBERT KURKA (1921-1957)

julius caesar

new york 2 march 1962	new yotk philharmonic	umpublished recording

FELIX LABUNSKI (1892-1979)

canto di aspirazione

new york 18 may 1969	american symphony	unpublished recording

EDOUARD LALO (1823-1892)

symphonie espagnole pour violon et orchestre

los angeles 2 september 1945	hollywood bowl symphony stern, violin	lp: kensington (usa) M 1030
los angeles 18 august 1946	hollywood bowl symphony totenberg, violin	unpublished recording
new york 5 january 1947	new york philharmonic thibaud, violin	lp: discocorp IGI 373 cd: theo van der burg (netherlands) cd: wing (japan) WCD 39

le roi d' ys, overture

los angeles 21 july 1946	hollywood bowl symphony	cd: enno riekena (germany)

JOSEPH LA MONACA

saltarello for piccolo and orchestra

philadelphia 27 october 1935	philadelphia orchestra fischer, piccolo	cd: cala CACD 0502 *unpublished victor 78rpm recording*

PAUL LAVALLE (1908-1997)

symphonic rumba

new york 6 december 1942	nbc symphony	unpublished recording

KURT LEIMER (1922-1974)

piano concerto no 2

saarbrücken 14-16 july 1969	saarbrücken radio orchestra leimer, piano	unpublished video recording

piano concerto no 4

new york 14 october 1956	symphony of the air leimer, piano	unpublished recording
new york march 1959	symphony of the air leimer, piano	lp: emi 1C063 29030 lp: gloria (japan) 12PAL 2100
saarbrücken 14-16 july 1969	saarbrücken radio orchestra leimer, piano	unpublished video recording

RUGGIERO LEONCAVALLO (1858-1919)

stridono lassu/i pagliacci

los angeles 26 august 1945	hollywood bowl symphony moffat	cd: enno riekena (germany)

ANATOL LIADOV (1885-1914)

chants populaires russes

camden nj 17 march 1934	philadelphia orchestra	78: victor 1681 and 8491 78: hmv DA 1415 and DB 2443 45: rca camden CAE 256 cd: pearl GEMMCD 9031 cd: iron needle IN 1334 cd: sirio 530010 cd: history 20.3290 *CAE 256 described performers as warwick so*
los angeles 22 july 1945	hollywood bowl symphony	cd: enno riekena (germany)
london 15 june 1969	royal philharmonic	cd: music and arts CD 847 cd: bbc legends BBCL 40692 *only 4 of the movements were played at this concert*

dance of the amazon

camden nj 8 december 1924	philadelphia orchestra	78: victor 1112 lp: british stokowski society LS 3

FRANZ LISZT (1811-1886)

piano concerto no 1

london 10 september 1966	new philharmonia rosen, piano	unpublished recording

hungarian fantasia for piano and orchestra

new york 8-10 march 1969	american symphony wild, piano	cd: theo van der burg (netherlands) *rehearsal was apparently also recorded*

les préludes, symphonic poem

los angeles 4 august 1946	hollywood bowl symphony	unpublished recording
new york 9 december 1947	his symphony orchestra	78: victor M 1277 45: victor WDM 1277 lp: victor LM 1073 lp: hmv (france) FALP 105 lp: hmv (italy) QALP 105 lp: british stokowski society LS 8 cd: cala CACD 0522

mephisto waltz

edinburgh 22 august 1961	london symphony	lp: japanese stokowski society JLSS 6-8 cd: bbc legends BBCL 40592

hungarian rhapsody no 1 in f minor

new york 10 february 1955	nbc symphony	lp: victor LM 1878 lp: victor (france) 630349 lp: quintessence PMC 7023 cd: theo van der burg (netherlands) cd: emi 575 4812 cd: cala awaiting publication

liszt/**hungarian rhapsody no 2 in c sharp minor**

camden nj 20 may 1920	philadelphia orchestra	78: victor 74647/6236
philadelphia 18 november 1926	philadelphia orchestra	78: victor 6652 78: hmv D 1296 78: hmv (italy) AW 4032 lp: victor VCM 7101/VIC 6060 cd: biddulph WHL 027 cd: grammofono AB 78552 cd: magic talent MT 48015 cd: magic masters MM 37022 cd: cantus classics 500.090 *recording completed on 10 march 1927*
philadelphia 16 november 1936	philadelphia orchestra	78: victor 14422 78: hmv DB 3086 cd: andante 2985
philadelphia 1937	philadelphia orchestra	film soundtrack recording *one hundred men and a girl*
new york july 1941	all-american symphony	78: columbia (usa) 11646 78: columbia (argentina) 264723
new york 9 february 1955	nbc symphony	lp: victor LM 1878 lp: victor (france) 630349 lp: quintessence PMC 7023 cd: theo van der burg (netherlands) cd: cala awaiting publication
new york 7 february 1961	rca victor symphony	lp: victor LM 2471/LSC 2471/VCS 7077/ AGL1-5259 lp: rca RB 16259/SB 2130 cd: rca/bmg 74321 709312/09026 615032/ 09026 626022/09026 685242
new york 6 october 1969	american symphony	unpublished recording

hungarian rhapsody no 3 in d

new york 13 january 1955	nbc symphony	lp: victor LM 1878 lp: victor (france) 630349 lp: quintessence PMC 7023 cd: theo van der burg (netherlands) cd: cala awaiting publication *recording completed on 9 february 1955*

NORMAN LOCKWOOD (1906-2002)

prairie

boston 19 november 1954	boston university orchestra and chorus	cd: enno riekena (germany)

CHARLES LOEFFLER (1861-1935)

a pagan poem

new york 18-20 december 1957	his symphony orchestra	lp: capitol P 8433/SP 8433 lp: angel seraphim 60080 cd: emi CDM 565 0742/567 5692

NICOLAI LOPATNIKOV (1903-1976)

symphony no 1

philadelphia 8 january 1932	philadelphia orchestra	bell telephone unpublished

OTTO LUENING (1900-1996)

pilgrims' hymn

new york 23 january 1949	new york philharmonic	unpublished recording

JEAN-BAPTISTE LULLY (1632-1935)

ballet suite

comprises movements from alceste, thésée and triomphe de l' amour

camden nj 30 april 1930	philadelphia orchestra	78: victor 7424 78: hmv DB 1587 lp: american stokowski society LSSA 5 cd: theo van der burg (netherlands) cd: music and arts CD 1173
new york 4 april 1952	his symphony orchestra	45: victor WDM 1721 lp: victor LM 1721/LM 1875 lp: hmv ALP 1387 cd: theo van der burg (netherlands) *LM 1875 and ALP 1387 contained notturno from triomphe de l' amour only*

GEORGE LYNN

gettysburg address

new york 21-22 may 1967	american symphony westminster choir kyser	unpublished recording

EDWARD MACDOWELL (1860-1908)

piano concerto no 2

new york 7 april 1942	nbc symphony nash, piano	cd: enno riekena (germany) *cd contains only first and second movements*
new york 20 november 1966	american symphony watts, piano	unpublished recording

suite no 2

camden nj december 1932	philadelphia orchestra	victor unpublished

GUSTAV MAHLER (1860-1911)

symphony no 2 "resurrection"

london 30 july 1963	london symphony goldsmiths, harrow and bbc choirs woodland baker	lp: penzance records PR 19 lp: japanese stokowski society JLSS 6-8 cd: intaglio INCD 7491 cd: music and arts CD 885 cd: bbc legends BBCL 41362
new york 3 april 1965	american symphony orchestra and choirs boatwright allen	unpublished rehearsal recording
philadelphia 3-9 november 1967	philadelphia orchestra singing city choir tyler godoy	cd: japanese stokowski society LSCD 26 cd: memories HR 4495-4497 cd: arkadia CDGI 749
new york 6 april 1971	american symphony westminster choir moody parker	unpublished recording
walthamstow 22-27 july 1974	london symphony lso chorus m.price fassbaender	lp: rca ARL2-0852/GL 85392 cd: rca/bmg 09026 625062/09026 684432 *rehearsal extracts* cd: rca/bmg 09026 684432 *recording completed on 14 august 1974*

mahler/**symphony no 8 "symphony of a thousand"**

new york 9 april 1950	new york philharmonic westminster choir schola cantorum yeend graf williams lipton bernhardt conley alexander london	lp: penzance records PR 19 lp: japanese stokowski society JLSS 6-8 cd: music and arts CD 280/CD 1130 cd: new york philharmonic NYP 9801-9812 cd: arkadia 78586/CDGI 761 cd: membran 222145 cd: archipel ARPCD 0108 *CD 280 was incorrectly dated 6 april 1950*

FRANK MARTIN (1890-1974)

petite symphonie concertante

new york 3-5 december 1957	his symphony orchestra	lp: capitol P 8507/SP 8507 lp: world records CM 69/SCM 69 cd: emi CDM 565 8682
new york 1 december 1962	american symphony	unpublished rehearsal recording
new york 18 april 1964	american symphony	unpublished rehearsal recording

harpsichord concerto

new york 21-23 october 1966	american symphony puyana, harpsichord	unpublished recording *rehearsal was apparently also recorded*

les 4 éléments

new york 16-20 may 1968	american symphony	unpublished recording *rehearsal was apparently also recorded*

JULES MASSENET (1842-1912)

gavotte/manon

los angeles 28 july 1946	hollywood bowl symphony connor	unpublished recording

WILLIAM MAYER (born 1925)

octagon for piano and orchestra

new york 23 march 1971	american symphony masselos, piano	unpublished recording

HARL MCDONALD (1899-1955)

rumba/symphony no 2

camden nj 25 november 1935	philadelphia orchestra	78: victor 8919 78: hmv DB 2913 lp: rca camden CAL 238 cd: japanese stokowski society LSCD 20 cd: cala CACD 0501 *CAL 238 named performers as warwick symphony*
philadelphia 8 december 1935	philadelphia orchestra	unpublished recording

concerto for 2 pianos and orchestra

philadelphia 19 april 1937	philadelphia orchestra behrend and kelberine, pianos	78: victor M 557 78: hmv DB 5700-5702 cd: japanese stokowski society LSCD 20 cd: cala CACD 0501 cd: history 205.652303

dance of the workers/festival of the workers

philadelphia 25 november 1935	philadelphia orchestra	78: victor 8919 78: hmv DB 2913 cd: japanese stokowski society LSCD 20 cd: cala CACD 0501

legend of the arkansas traveller

philadelphia 27 march 1940	philadelphia orchestra hilsberg, violin	78: victor 18069 lp: rca camden CAL 238 cd: japanese stokowski society LSCD 20 cd: cala CACD 0501 *CAL 238 named performers as warwick symphony*

GEORGE FREDERICK MCKAY (1899-1970)

evocation/from a moonlit ceremony

los angeles 18 august 1946	hollywood bowl symphony	unpublished recording

COLIN MCPHEE (1900-1960)

nocturne for chamber orchestra

new york 3 december 1958	contemptary music society	unpublished recording

tabuh-tabuhan

new york 16 october 1953	his symphony orchestra	cd: enno riekena (germany)

FELIX MENDELSSOHN-BARTHOLDY (1809-1847)

symphony no 3 "scotch"

new york 26 october 1947	new york philharmonic	cd: new york philharmonic NYP 9701 *second movement* cd: new york philharmonic NYP 9712

symphony no 4 "italian"

london 31 may- 4 june 1977	national philharmonic	lp: cbs 34567/76673 cd: sony MBK 39498/MBK 44894 cd: bella musica 31.6007/BMF 966 *stokowski's final recording sessions; bella musica editions incorrectly dated 1950*

mendelssohn/**a midsummer night's dream, overture**

new york 21-23 december 1968	american symphony	unpublished recording *rehearsal was apparently also recorded*

scherzo/a midsummer night's dream

camden nj 8 november 1917	philadelphia orchestra	78: victor 74560/6238
philadelphia 4 december 1931	philadelphia orchestra	bell telephone unpublished
philadelphia 5 december 1931	philadelphia orchestra	lp: bell telephone laboratories BTL 7901 cd: iron needle IN 1402 cd: theo van der burg (netherlands)
new york 11 july 1941	all-american symphony	78: columbia (usa) 11983 cd: music and arts CD 845
los angeles 25 august 1946	hollywood bowl symphony	lp: japanese stokowski society JLSS 6-8 cd: enno riekena (germany)

wedding march/a midsummer night's dream

camden nj march 1923	philadelphia orchestra	victor unpublished

ruy blas, overture

new york 7 may 1966	american symphony	cd: theo van der burg (netherlands) *this was a rehearsal performance*

PETER MENNIN (1923-1983)

symphony no 3

new york 5 december 1964	american symphony	unpublished recording

moby dick concerto

new york 23 february 1963	american symphony	unpublished rehearsal recording

canto

new york 25-26 february 1967	american symphony	unpublished recording *rehearsal was apparently also recorded*

DARIUS MILHAUD (1892-1974)

symphony no 1

new york 21 march 1943	nbc symphony	unpublished recording

concerto for percussion and small orchestra

baden-baden 15 may 1955	swf orchestra	cd: music and arts CD 778

saudades do brasil no 2

los angeles 13 august 1946	hollywood bowl symphony	unpublished recording

SHUKICHI MITSUKURI (1895-1971)

10 haikus by basho

new york 3 december 1958	contemporary music society	unpublished recording

SHARON MOE

fanfare

new york 25-26 march 1972	american symphony	unpublished recording *rehearsal was apparently also recorded*

RICHARD MOHAUPT (1904-1957)

concerto on russian army songs

new york 19 december 1943	nbc symphony	unpublished recording

ITALO MONTEMEZZI (1875-1952)

la mia italia

los angeles 30 july 1946	hollywood bowl symphony	unpublished recording

CLAUDIO MONTEVERDI (1567-1643)

vespro della beata vergine, abridged version

illinois 12 november 1952	university orchestra and choirs stewart clark miller foote	lp: university of illinois custom recording CRS 1 cd: rediscovery RD 16

DOUGLAS MOORE (1893-1969)

polka and cakewalk from the cotillon suite

new york 25 october 1953	cbs studio orchestra	cd: enno riekena (germany)

FRANCOIS MOREL (born 1926)

antiphonie

new york 16 october 1953	his symphony orchestra	cd: enno riekena (germany)

WOLFGANG AMADEUS MOZART (1756-1791)

symphony no 25

houston 18-19 october 1959	houston symphony	unpublished recording

symphony no 35 "haffner"

new york 20 november 1949	new york philharmonic	lp: japanese stokowski society JLSS 15 cd: theo van der burg (netherlands) cd: cala CACD 0537 *japanese stokowski society issue was incorrectly dated 5 november 1949*

symphony no 40

camden nj 9 may 1919	philadelphia orchestra	78: victor 74609/6243 78: hmv DB 385 lp: british stokowski society LS 3 *this recording comprised third movement only*
new york 5 march 1960	new york philharmonic	unpublished recording
new york 23 march 1969	american symphony	unpublished recording *rehearsal was apparently also recorded*

symphony no 41 "jupiter"

los angeles 28 august 1946	hollywood bowl symphony	cd: theo van der burg (netherlands)
new york 23-24 april 1971	american symphony	unpublished recording *rehearsal was apparently also recorded*

piano concerto no 14

new york 2 november 1947	new york philharmonic hess, piano	cd: theo van der burg (netherlands)

mozart/**piano concerto no 20**

geneva 30 august 1969	international festival youth orchestra di carla, piano	lp: audio visual enterprises AVE 30696

piano concerto no 21

new york 6 february 1949	new york philharmonic hess, piano	lp: private edition recordings MJA 1967 cd: music and arts CD 779 cd: wing (japan) WCD 46 cd: theo van der burg (netherlands)

piano concerto no 24

houston 24-25 october 1960	houston symphony rachlin, piano	unpublished recording

concerto for flute and harp

philadelphia 21 november 1931	philadelphia orchestra kincaid, flute phillips, harp	bell telephone unpublished
washington 17 december 1955	national symphony mann, flute meyer, harp	unpublished recording

andante and rondo for flute and orchestra

new york 18-19 january 1970	american symphony rampal, flute	unpublished recording

serenade no 6 for four orchestras

new york 23 october 1949	new york philharmonic	unpublished recording

serenade no 10 for 13 wind instruments

washington 17 december 1955	national symphony	unpublished recording *only first and fifth movements were performed at this concert*
new york 25-27 may 1966	american symphony	lp: vanguard VRS 1158/VSD 71158/ VSD 707-708 lp: world records T 898/ST 898 cd: vanguard OVC 8009/08.00971

mozart/**sinfonia concertante for wind**

philadelphia 22 december 1940	philadelphia orchestra	78: victor M 760 78: hmv DB 10118-10121 lp: rca camden CAL 213/CFL 105 cd: history 205.652203 cd: cala CACD 0523 *CAL 213 described performers as warwick symphony orchestra*
new york 9 november 1963	american symphony	unpublished rehearsal recording
philadelphia 4 february 1964	philadelphia orchestra	unpublished recording
boston 6 march 1964	boston symphony	unpublished recording
tanglewood 21 august 1964	boston symphony	cd: theo van der burg (netherlands)

adagio and fugue in c minor

new york 22 february 1964	american symphony	unpublished recording

german dance no 3 "sleigh ride"

new york 2 march 1950	his symphony orchestra	78: victor 10-1487 45: victor 49-0553/ERA 119 lp: victor LM 1238 lp: british stokowski society LS 18 cd: theo van der burg (netherlands) cd: cala CACD 0532

turkish march/piano sonata no 11

new york 9 february 1955	nbc symphony	lp: victor LM 2042 lp: british stokowski society LS 18 lp: japanese stokowski society JLSS 17 cd: theo van der burg (netherlands) cd: cala CACD 0543 *original issue may have named orchestra as his symphony orchestra*

mozart/**don giovanni, overture**

los angeles 30 july 1946	hollywood bowl symphony	unpublished recording
boston 13 january 1968	boston symphony	cd: boston symphony orchestra CB 101-112
west ham march 1976	national philharmonic	lp: pye nixa PCNHX 6 lp: dell' arte DA 9003 lp: vogue CV 25013 cd: pye nixa CDPCN 6 cd: emi CDM 764 1402

le nozze di figaro, overture

philadelphia 12 february 1960	philadelphia orchestra	lp: japanese stokowski society JLSS 1-2 cd: theo van der burg (netherlands)
new york 23 february 1963	american symphony	unpublished rehearsal recording
new york 9-10 january 1966	american symphony	unpublished recording
london 30 september 1973	royal philharmonic	unpublished recording

dove sono/le nozze di figaro

los angeles 26 august 1945	hollywood bowl symphony moffat	cd: enno riekena (germany)

non piu andrai/le nozze di figaro

los angeles 19 august 1945	hollywood bowl symphony moscona	unpublished recording
philadelphia 20 january 1962	philadelphia orchestra london	lp: melodram MEL 228 cd: di stefano GDS 2204 cd: bella voce BLV 107.235

mozart/**die zauberflöte, overture**

new york 23 march 1971	american symphony	unpublished recording

missa brevis k65

washington 17 december 1955	national symphony howard university choir	unpublished recording *only three movements of the mass were performed at this concert*

ave verum corpus

washington 17 devember 1955	national symphony howard university choir	unpublished recording

kyrie k341

washington 17 december 1955	national symphony howard university choir	unpublished recording

alleluja/exsultate jubilate

philadelphia 1937	philadelphia orchestra durbin	film soundtrack recording *one hundred men and a girl*

MODEST MUSSORGSKY (1839-1881)

pictures at an exhibition

philadelphia 12 march 1932	philadelphia orchestra	lp: bell telephone laboratories BTL 7901 cd: iron needle IN 1402 *extracts only were played for this recording*
philadelphia 27 november 1939	philadelphia orchestra	78: victor M 706 78: hmv DB 5827-5830 78: hmv (australia) ED 209-212 lp: british stokowski society LS 14 cd: history 20.3290 cd: dutton CDAX 8009
new york july 1941	all-american symphony	78: columbia (usa) M 511 78: columbia (canada) 15639-15642 78: columbia (argentina) 266059-266062
new york 21 march 1943	nbc symphony	unpublished recording
philadelphia 16 march 1962	philadelphia orchestra	cd: japanese stokowski society LSCD 23-24
london 23 july 1963	bbc symphony	cd: music and arts CD 765 cd: seven seas (japan) KICC 2076 *great gate of kiev* cd: japanese stokowski society LSCD 23-24
london 15 september 1965	new philharmonia	lp: decca LK 4766/PFS 4095/SDD 456/ SPA 159/VIV 26 lp: decca (germany) 642.743 lp: london (usa) PM 55004/SPC 21006/ STS 15558 cd: castle classics CCD 107 cd: decca 436 5312/443 8982/467 8282
new york 21 october 1965	american symphony	unpublished rehearsal recording
new york 4 may 1969	american symphony	cd: theo van der burg (netherlands)
houston 19-20 october 1969	houston symphony	unpublished recording

mussorgsky/**hut on fowl's legs and great gate of kiev/pictures at an exhibition**

new york 22 january 1957	his symphony orchestra	lp: capitol P 8385/P 8694/SP 8694 lp: angel seraphim 6094 cd: emi CDM 565 6142 *recording completed on 29 january 1957*

boris godunov, symphonic synthesis

philadelphia 16 november 1936	philadelphia orchestra	78: victor M 391 78: hmv DB 3244-3246 lp: rca camden CAL 140 lp: british stokowski society LS 14 cd: dutton CDAX 8009 cd: andante 4978 *CAL 140 named performers as warwick symphony*
new york 4-5 july 1941	all-american symphony	78: columbia (usa) M 516 78: columbia (brazil) 30.5276-5278
new york 14 april 1942	nbc symphony	unpublished recording
new york 18 december 1966	american symphony	unpublished recording
boston 13 january 1968	boston symphony	cd: memories HR 4495-4497
montreux 11 september 1968	orchestre de la suisse romande	cd: theo van der burg (netherlands)
geneva 12 september 1968	orchestre de la suisse romande	lp: decca PFS 4181/SDD 456/SPA 142 lp: london (usa) SPC 21032/SPC 21110 lp: musical heritage society MHS 827052 cd: castle classics CCD 107 cd: decca 443 8962/475 6090
philadelphia 13 february 1969	philadelphia orchestra	unpublished recording *recording made at stokowski's final public concert with philadelphia orchestra*
new york 9-10 march 1969	american symphony	cd: theo van der burg (netherlands)
new york 6 october 1969	american symphony hines	unpublished recording

mussorgsky/**night on bare mountain**

philadelphia april 1939	philadelphia orchestra	*fantasia soundtrack recording* lp: top rank 30-003 lp: disneyland WDL 4101/ST 3926/STER 101 lp: buena vista BVS 101 cd: buena vista CD 020/60007 cd: pony canyon PCCD 00009 cd: avex AVCW 12048-12049/12163-12164 cd: pickwick DSTCD 452 vhs video: buena vista D 211322 vhs video: disneyland 101 dvd video: disney classics ZIDD 888113/888055
philadelphia 8 december 1940	philadelphia orchestra	78: victor 17900 78: hmv DB 5900 78: hmv (australia) ED 168 45: victor 49-0722 lp: victor VCM 7101 lp: rca camden CAL 118 lp: british stokowski society LS 14 cd: dutton CDAX 8009 cd: pearl GEMMCD 9488 cd: grammofono AB 78586 cd: magic talent MT 48002 cd: magic masters MM 37022 cd: phonographe PH 5025-5026 cd: history 20.3290 cd: documents 221708 *CAL 118 named performers as warwick symphony*
new york february 1953	his symphony orchestra	lp: victor LM 1816 lp: victor (france) 630215 lp: quintessence PMC 7026 cd: theo van der burg (netherlands)
london 17 september 1964	london symphony	cd: music and arts CD 765/CD 657 cd: seven seas (japan) KICC 2076
london 15 june 1967	london symphony	unpublished recording
london 16 june 1967	london symphony	lp: decca LK 4927/PFS 4139/PFS 4260/SDD 456 lp: london (usa) SPC 21026/SPC 21110 lp: musical heritage society MHS 827052 lp: franklin mint 23 lp: readers' digesr RDS 9019/GMEL 8A-S9 cd: castle classics CCD 107/pickwick IMPX 9033 cd: decca 430 1372/430 4122/430 4162/ 433 6252/443 8962/475 6090
london 15 june 1969	royal philharmonic	cd: music and arts CD 847 cd: bbc legends BBCL 40692

mussorgsky/khovantschina, entr' acte

camden nj 12 december 1922	philadelphia orchestra	78: victor 74803/6336 78: hmv DB 599
philadelphia 12 october 1927	philadelphia orchestra	78: victor M 53 78: hmv D 1427 lp: british stokowski society LS 14 cd: grammofono AB 78552 cd: nuova era HMT 90017/PH 5001 cd: dutton CDAX 8009 cd: sirio 53.0021 cd: history 20.3290 cd: andante 4978
los angeles 23 july 1946	hollywood bowl symphony	unpublished recording
new york 14 april 1953	his symphony orchestra	lp: victor LM 1816 lp: victor (france) 630215 lp: quintessence PMC 7026 cd: rediscovery RD 009 cd: theo van der burg (netherlands)
stuttgart 20 may 1955	sdr orchestra	cd: refrain (japan) DR 930051
london 10 september 1966	new philharmonia	unpublished recording
philadelphia 14 october 1966	philadelphia orchestra	unpublished recording
budapest 2 february 1967	hungarian state orchestra	cd: theo van der burg (netherlands)
copenhagen 4 august 1967	danish radio orchestra	unpublished recording
new york 7-9 may 1972	american symphony	cd: venezia (japan) V 1004
west ham november 1975	national philharmonic	45: nimbus 45204 lp: pye nixa PCNHX 4 lp: vogue CV 25013 cd: pye nixa CDPCN 4

mussorgsky/**khovantschina, ptelude and dance of the persian slaves**

new york 26 february 1953	his symphony orchestra	lp: victor LM 1816 lp: victor (france) 630215 lp: quintessence PMC 7026

boris godunov, scenes from the opera

san francisco 8-10 december 1952	san francisco symphony and opera chorus rossi-lemeni mason cauwet	45: victor WDM 1764 lp: victor LM 1764 lp: dell' arte DA 9002 cd: theo van der burg (netherlands) cd: cala CACD 0535 *excerpts* lp: grandi voci GVS 17 *rehearsal extract* cd: archive documents ADCD 200-201

parassia's dream/sorochinsky fair

los angeles 22 july 1945	hollywood bowl symphony koshetz	cd: eklipse EKRCD 31 cd: bella voce BLV 107.235 cd: enno riekena (germany)

song of the flea

los angeles 25 august 1946	hollywood bowl symphony ford *sung in english*	cd: enno riekena (germany)

CARL NIELSEN (1865-1931)

symphony no 2 "four temperaments"

copenhagen 4 august 1967	danish radio orchestra	lp: poco PLP 8407 cd: theo van der burg (netherlands) cd: emi 575 4812

symphony no 6 "sinfonia semplice"

london 10 september 1965	new philharmonia	cd: bbc legends BBCL 40592 *incorrectly dated 12 september 1967*

OTTOKAR NOVACEK (1966-1900)

perpetuum mobile

philadelphia 8 december 1940	philadelphia orchestra	78: victor 18069 lp: rca camden CAL 123 cd: biddulph WHL 047 *CAL 123 names performers as warwick symphony*
new york 5 july 1941	all-american symphony	78: columbia (usa) 11879
new york 6 february 1944	nbc symphony	unpublished recording
london 17 september 1964	london symphony	unpublished recording
west ham july 1976	national philharmonic	lp: cbs 34543/73589 cd: cala CACD 0529

JACQUES OFFENBACH (1819-1880)

barcarolle/les contes d' hoffmann

los angeles july 1945	hollywood bowl symphony	78: victor 11-9174/M 1062 78: hmv DB 10130 lp: rca camden CAL 153 *CAL 153 names performers as star symphony*

orfée aux enfers, overture

los angeles 25 august 1946	hollywood bowl symphony	lp: japanese stokowski society JLSS 6-8 cd: enno riekena (germany)

MICHAL KLEOFAS OGINSKI (1765-1833)

polish national hymn

new york 10 december 1966	american symphony	unpublished recording

JUAN ORREGO-SALAS (born 1919)

obertura festiva

new york 25 september 1958	his symphony orchestra	unpublished recording

CARL ORFF (1895-1982)

carmina burana

boston 19 november 1954	boston university orchestra and chorus tobin, belle, dickey	cd: enno riekena (germany)
rome 30 april 1955	rai roma orchestra and chorus tuccari, pirino, oppicelli	unpublished recording
houston 9-13 april 1958	houston symphony houston chorale babikian hager gardner	lp: capitol P 8470/SP 8470 lp: angel seraphim 60236 lp: world records T 793/ST 793 lp: emi CFP 40311/2C053 81104 cd: emi CDM 565 2072/253 8442/567 5692 cd: theorema TH 121.144
new york 7 may 1966	american symphony orchestra and chorus parrett, nason, gwynne	cd: theo van der burg (netherlands) *this was a rehearsal performance*
new york 18 may 1969	american symphony westminster choir hoagland, murphy, mosley	unpublished recording

a midsummer night's dream, incidental music to the play

new york 20 july 1956	symphony of the air and chorus rathbone, buttons, wickwire, wilson	unpublished recording

IGNAZ JAN PADEREWSKI (1860-1941)

piano concerto in a minor

new york 6-11 october 1970	american symphony wild, piano	cd: theo van der burg (netherlands)

NICCOLO PAGANINI (1782-1840)

violin concerto no 1

new york 27 april 1970	american symphony maehashi, violin	unpublished recording

moto perpetuo

los angeles 11 august 1946	hollywood bowl symphony	unpublished recording
new york 15-17 august 1957	his symphony orchestra	lp: capitol P 8415/P 8650/SP 8415/ SP 8650 lp: emi SXLP 30174 cd: emi CDM 565 9122

GIOVANNI PALESTRINA (1524-1594)

adoramus te

camden nj 12 november 1934	philadelphia orchestra	78: victor M 508/M 963 78: hmv DA 1606/DB 6260 lp: american stokowski society LSSA 5 cd: theo van der burg (netherlands) cd: music and arts CD 1173
new york 4 april 1952	unaccompanied chorus	45: victor WDM 1721 lp: victor LM 1721 lp: quintessence PMC 7110
new york 15 december 1958	symphony of the air	lp: united artists UAL 7001/UAS 8001/ UAS 8003 cd: emi CMS 565 4272
philadelphia 13 february 1969	philadelphia orchestra	unpublished recording

o bone jesu

new york 26 march 1952	unaccompanied chorus	45: victor WDM 1721 lp: victor LM 1721

ANDRZEJ PANUFNIK (1914-1991)

sinfonia sacra

new york 12 devember 1966	american symphony	unpublished recording

symphony for peace

detroit 17 february 1955	detroit symphony lutnia singing society	unpublished recording

universal prayer

london 4-5 september 1970	halsey singers cantelo watts mitchinson stalman	lp: unicorn RHS 305/DKP 9049 cd: theo van der burg (netherlands)
twickenham 20 june 1971	halsey singers cantelo watts partridge stalman	unpublished video recording

katyn epitaph

new york 16-18 november 1968	american symphony	unpublished recording *rehearsal was apparently also recorded*

ODON PARTOS (1907-1977)

yizkor for viola and orchestra

new york 3 december 1958	contemporary music society zaratzian, viola	unpublished recording

PEKKO

music from janucz

los angeles 4 august 1946	hollywood bowl symphony	unpublished recording

VINCENT PERSICHETTI (1915-1987)

march from the divertimento for band

new york 22 january 1957	his symphony orchestra	lp: capitol P 8385 lp: angel seraphim 6094 cd: emi CDM 565 6142 *recording completed on 29 january 1957*

the hollow men, for trumpet and strings

philadelphia 21 june 1965	philadelphia orchestra	unpublished recording

WALTER PISTON (1894-1976)

concerto for orchestra

new york 18 april 1966	american symphony	unpublished recording

fantasy for cor anglais, harp and strings

new york 14 march 1954	cbs studio orchestra	cd: theo van der burg (netherlands)

divertimento for 9 instruments

new york 3 december 1958	contemporary music society	unpublished recording

AMILCARE PONCHIELLI (1834-1886)

dance of the hours/la gioconda

philadelphia april 1939	philadelphia orchestra	*fantasia soundtrack recording* lp: top rank 30-003 lp: disneyland WDL 4101/ST 3926/STER 101 lp: buena vista BVS 101 cd: buena vista CD 020/60007 cd: pony canyon PCCD 00009 cd: avex AVCW 12048-12049/12163-12164 cd: pickwick DSTCD 452 vhs video: buena vista D 211322 vhs video: disneyland 101 dvd video: ZIDD 888113/ZIDD 888055

DAVID POPPER (1843-1913)

cello concerto

new york 14-17 november 1970	american symphony silberstein, cello	unpublished recording *rehearsal was apparently also recorded*

ENNIO PORRINO (1910-1959)

nuraghi

rome 3 may 1953	santa cecilia orchestra	unpublished recording

FRANCIS POULENC (1899-1963)

concert champetre for harpsichord and orchestra

new york 19 november 1949	new york philharmonic landowska, harpsichord	lp: international piano archives IPA 106-107 lp: columbia (japan) DXM 153-154 cd: dante LYS 482 cd: music and arts CD 821
new york 23 february 1963	american symphony marlowe, harpsichord	unpublished rehearsal recording

MICHAEL PRAETORIUS (1571-1621)

es ist ein ros entsprungen

new york 29 december 1971	american symphony saint patrick's choir valente *sung in english*	unpublished recording

SERGEI PROKOFIEV (1891-1953)

symphony no 5

moscow 15 june 1957	ussr large radio orchestra	lp: artia MK 1551/MK 4408 lp: bruno BR 14050 cd: theo van der burg (netherlands)
new york 25-26 february 1967	american symphony	unpublished recording *rehearsal was apparently also recorded*

symphony no 6

new york 26 november- 4 december 1949	new york philharmonic	lp: new york philharmonic NYP 821-822 lp: japanese stokowski society JLSS 16 cd: theo van der burg (netherlands)

piano concerto no 2

new york 10-12 october 1971	american symphony bolet, piano	cd: theo van der burg (netherlands) *rehearsal was apparently also recorded*

piano concerto no 3

new york 20 february 1949	new york philharmonic kapell, piano	lp: melodram MEL 228 cd: music and arts CD 769/CD 990 *MEL 228 incorrectly named orchestra as nbc symphony; CD 990 incorrectly dated 5 march 1949*

violin concerto no 2

new york 9-10 january 1966	american symphony senofsky, violin	unpublished recording

sinfonia concertante for cello and orchestra

new york 14 december 1969	american symphony gutman, cello	cd: theo van der burg (netherlands)

l' amour des 3 oranges, suite from the opera

new york 18 november 1941	nbc symphony	cd: enno riekena (germany) *also includes spoken introduction by stokowski*
new york 27 november 1941	nbc symphony	78: victor 18497 78: hmv DB 6151/DB 11130 lp: american stokowski society LSSA 4 cd: theo van der burg (netherlands) *march only* cd: cala CACD 0505

prokofiev/**alexander nevsky, cantata**

new york 7 march 1943	nbc symphony westminster choir tourel *sung in english*	cd: enno riekena (germany) *this was the american premiere performance of the work*
new york 24 february 1964	american symphony rutgers university choir rankin	cd: theo van der burg (netherlands) *this was a rehearsal performance*
philadelphia 19-21 june 1965	philadelphia orchestra and chorus bonazzi	unpublished recording *rehearsal was apparently also recorded*
new york 16 may 1968	american symphony dessoff choir	unpublished rehearsal recording
amsterdam 20-22 august 1970	radio philharmonic orchestra and chorus sante	cd: music and arts CD 252/CD 831 *excerpt* cd: byton studios SVS 9502 *also unpublished video recording*

cinderella, suite from the ballet

new york 8 october 1958	new york philharmonic	lp: everest LPBR 6016/LPBR 6108/ SDBR 3016/SDBR 3108 lp: world records T 173/ST 173 lp: concert hall SMSC 2533 cd: bescol CD 519 cd: priceless D 22697 cd: everest EVC 9023 *orchestra described for this recording as stadium symphony orchestra*

lieutenant kijé, suite from the incidental music

los angeles august 1946	hollywood bowl symphony	cd: theo van der burg (netherlands)

the ugly duckling

new york 3 october 1958	new york philharmonic resnik, narrator	lp: everest LPBR 6108/SDBR 3108 lp: world records T 173/ST 173 cd: bescol CD 519 cd: everest EVC 9023 cd: legacy 359 *orchestra described for this recording as stadium symphony orchestra*

prokofiev/**peter and the wolf**

new york july 1941	all-american symphony rathbone, narrator	78: columbia (usa) M 477 78: columbia (canada) 15522-15524 78: columbia (argentina) 266063-266065 lp: columbia (usa) ML 4038/CL 671/P 14204 cd: avid AMSC 601
new york 3 october 1958	new york philharmonic keeshan, narrator	lp: everest LPBR 6043/SDBR 3043 cd: everest EVC 9048 cd: bescol CD 519 cd: mode laser 670027 *orchestra described for this recording as stadium symphony; mode laser edition has french language narration*

romeo and juliet, suite from the ballet

new york 5-7 october 1954	nbc symphony	lp: victor LM 2117/LM 6028/ARL1-2715 cd: rca/bmg 74321 709312/09026 625172/ 09026 684432
baden-baden 15 may 1955	swf orchestra	cd: music and arts CD 831
chicago 9 january 1958	chicago symphony	unpublished recording

GIACOMO PUCCINI (1858-1924)

si mi chiamano mimi/la boheme

los angeles	hollywood bowl	unpublished recording
28 july	symphony	
1946	connor	

quando m' en vo/la boheme

los angeles	hollywood bowl	unpublished recording
28 july	symphony	
1946	connor	

madama butterfly, entr' acte

camden nj	philadelphia	victor unpublished
december	orchestra	
1924		

recondita armonia/tosca

philadelphia	philadelphia	cd: bella voce BLV 107.235
19 january	orchestra	
1963	corelli	

vissi d' arte/tosca

philadelphia	philadelphia	lp: melodram MEL 228
20 january	orchestra	cd: bella voce BLV 107.235
1962	nilsson	cd: shinchosa (japan) 00612

turandot

new york	metropolitan	lp: metropolitan opera special edition
4 march	opera orchestra	lp: historic recording enterprises HRE 229
1961	and chorus	lp: melodram MEL 048
	nilsson	lp: accord ACC 15.0038
	moffo	cd: metropolitan opera MET 16
	corelli	cd: datum 12301
	giaiotti	cd: memories HR 4535-4536
	guarrera	cd: shinchosa (japan) 00612
		excerpts
		lp: melodram MEL 099

HENRY PURCELL (1658-1695)

when i am laid in earth/dido and aeneas

new york 25 july 1950	his symphony otchestra	78: victor 12-3087 45: victor 49-3087 lp: victor LM 1875 lp: hmv ALP 1387 cd: theo van der burg (netherlands)
london 7 may 1954	bbc symphony	vhs video: teldec 4509 950383 laserdisc: teldec 4509 950386 dvd video: teldec 0927 426672 *bbc television*
london 16-19 august 1975	royal philharmonic	lp: desmar DSM 1011 lp: decca (germany) 642.631 cd: emi 566 7602

hornpipe/king arthur

new york 10 february 1958	his symphony orchestra	lp: capitol P 8458/SP 8458 lp: angel seraphim 6094 cd: emi CDM 565 9122 *recording completed on 19 and 26 february 1958*

symphony/the fairy queen

london 7 may 1954	bbc symphony	unpublished video recording *bbc television*

SERGEI RACHMANINOV (1873-1943)

symphony no 2

los angeles 13 august 1946	hollywood bowl symphony	lp: discocorp/american stokowski society LSSA 28 cd: music and arts CD 769

a new recording of the symphony was planned at the time of stokowski's death in 1977

symphony no 3

west ham 28 april- 1 may 1975	national philharmonic	lp: desmar DES 1007/DSM 1007 lp: decca (germany) 642.613 cd: emi 566 7592

rachmaninov/**piano concerto no 2**

camden nj december 1923- december 1924	philadelphia orchestra rachmaninov, piano	78: victor 89166-89171/8064-8066 78: hmv DB 747-749 lp: victor ARM3-0260 cd: rca/bmg 09026 612652 *78rpm editions contained only second and third movements of the concerto; lp and cd editions replaced missing sections of the recording with appropriate sections from the 1929 recording*
philadelphia 10-13 april 1929	philadelphia orchestra rachmaninov, piano	78: victor M 58 78: hmv DB 1333-1337/DB 7427-7431 45: victor WCT 18 lp: victor LCT 1014/LSB 4011/ARM3-0296 lp: hmv ALP 1630/CSLP 517 lp: rca AVM 30296/VL 42058 lp: international piano archives IPA 276 cd: pickwick PK 524 cd: rca/bmg 09026 612652 cd: biddulph LHW 036 cd: history 20.3290 cd: naxos 811.0601 *biddulph edition also includes alternative takes*
los angeles 1 august 1945	hollywood bowl symphony rubinstein, piano	cd: biddulph LHW 041

piano concerto no 3

prague 20 may 1961	czech philharmonic oborin, piano	cd: andante AN 2150

symphonic dances

houston 19-20 october 1959	houston symphony	unpublished recording

the isle of the dead

los angeles 23 july 1946	hollywood bowl symphony	cd: pearl GEMMCD 9261

3 russian songs

new york 18 december 1966	american symphony schola cantorum	unpublished recording

rachmaninov/**rhapsody on a theme of paganini**

camden nj 24 december 1934	philadelphia orchestra rachmaninov, piano	78: victor M 250 78: hmv DB 2426-2428 45: victor WCT 1118 lp: victor LCT 1118/LSB 4013/ARM3-0296 lp: hmv CSLP 509 cd: pickwick PK 524 cd: rca/bmg 09026 612652 cd: fidelio 8822-3EB3 cd: monopoly GI 2030 cd: membran 222174 cd: history 205.652303 cd: naxos 811.0602
philadelphia 19 january 1963	philadelphia orchestra starr, piano	cd: theo van der burg (netherlands)
new york 3 february 1968	american symphony lewenthal, piano	unpublished video recording *rehearsal was apparently also recorded*
london 25 april 1973	london symphony vered, piano	unpublished recording

georgian melody

los angeles 22 july 1945	hollywood bowl symphony koshetz	cd: eklipse EKRCD 31 cd: enno riekena (germany) cd: bella voce BLV 107.235

prelude in c sharp minor

philadelphia 17 december 1962	philadelphia orchestra	lp: discocorp/american stokowski society LSSA 28
prague 7-8 september 1972	czech philharmonic	lp: decca PFS 4351 lp: london (usa) SPC 21130 cd: decca 433 8762/475 1452

rachmaninov/**vocalise**

new york 25 february 1953	his symphony orchestra	lp: victor LM 2042 lp: british stokowski society LS 17 lp: japanese stokowski society JLSS 14 cd: theo van der burg (netherlands) cd: cala CACD 0542
new york 15-17 august 1957	his symphony orchestra	lp: capitol P 8415/P 8650/SP 8415/ SP 8650 lp: angel seraphim 60278 lp: emi SXLP 30174 cd: emi CDM 565 9122
london 19-20 july 1961	new symphony luboff choir	cd: rca/bmg 09026 625992/09026 636692 *unpublished victor lp recording*
new york 14 april 1964	american symphony moffo	lp: victor LSC 2795/LSB 4114/VICS 1673 lp: rca SB 6804/AGL1-4877/GL 42923 cd: rca/bmg GD 87831/09026 626002
west ham 28 april- 1 may 1975	national philharmonic	lp: desmar DES 1007/DSM 1007 lp: decca (germany) 642.613 cd: emi 566 7592

GUENTER RAPHAEL (1903-1960)

jabonah

hamburg 7 july 1952	ndr orchestra	cd: enno riekena (germany) cd: tahra TAH 485-486

MAURICE RAVEL (1875-1937)

pavane pour une infante défunte

new york 18 april 1966	american symphony	unpublished recording

fanfare/l'éventail de jeanne

hilversum 24-25 august 1970	netherlands radio philharmonic	lp: decca PFS 4218 lp: london (usa) SPC 21061 cd: cala CACD 0525 cd: decca 475 1452

ravel/**alboroda del gracioso**

los angeles 1 september 1946	hollywood bowl symphony	unpublished recording
paris 12 may 1958	orchestre national	cd: music and arts CD 778
paris 13-15 may 1958	orchestre national	lp: capitol P 8463/P 8694/SP 8694 lp: angel seraphim 60102 lp: emi SXLP 30263 cd: emi CDC 747 4232/CDM 565 4222
moscow 7 june 1958	ussr large radio orchestra	unpublished recording
philadelphia 17 december 1962	philadelphia orchestra	unpublished recording

boléro

new york 26 july 1940	all-american symphony	78: columbia (usa) X 174 cd: music and arts CD 841 cd: history 205.652303
new york 3 february 1968	american symphony	unpublished recording
new york 4 may 1969	american symphony	unpublished recording

ravel/**daphnis et chloé, second suite**

new york 21 february 1943	nbc symphony	unpublished recording
new york february 1945	new york city symphony	unpublished recording
los angeles 12 august 1945	hollywood bowl symphony	cd: enno riekena (germany)
london 10 september 1966	new philharmonia	unpublished recording
london 20 june 1970	london symphony	unpublished recording
london 22-23 june 1970	london symphony	lp: decca PFS 4220/414 5001 lp: london (usa) SPC 21059/SPC 21112 cd: decca 417 7792/455 1522/475 1452

la valse

los angeles 18 august 1946	hollywood bowl symphony	unpublished recording
new york 16 march 1947	new york philharmonic	unpublished recording

tzigane pour violon et orchestre

los angeles 14 july 1946	hollywood bowl symphony wicks, violin	lp: musenkranz GMV 13Y

schéhérazade

new york 3 april 1967	american symphony godoy	unpublished recording

ravel/rapsodie espagnole

camden nj 17 march 1934	philadelphia orchestra	78: victor 8282-8283 78: hmv DB 2367-2368 lp: rca camden CAL 118 lp: neiman marcus (usa) cd: biddulph WHL 013 cd: pearl GEMMCD 9283 cd: history 205.652303 cd: andante 4978 *CAL 118 named performers as warwick symphony orchestra*
london 24 june 1957	london symphony	lp: capitol P 8520/SP 8520 lp: angel seraphim 60104 cd: emi CDC 747 4232/CDM 565 4222 *recording completed on 3 july 1957*
warsaw may 1959	warsaw philharmonic	cd: tvp TCD 014
leipzig 1 june 1959	gewandhaus orchestra	cd: music and arts CD 280
houston 24-25 october 1960	houston symphony	unpublished recording
new york 19 november 1967	american symphony	unpublished recording
london 14 may 1974	new philharmonia	cd: bbc radio classics BBCRD 9107 cd: nippon crown (japan) CRBC 6017

OTTORINO RESPIGHI (1879-1936)

pini di roma

los angeles 19 august 1945	hollywood bowl symphony	unpublished recording
houston 12 march 1957	houston symphony	unpublished recording
new york 15 december 1958	symphony of the air	lp: united artists UAL 7001/UAS 8001 cd: emi CMS 565 4272/CDM 565 9212
london 30 june 1959	london symphony	unpublished recording
philadelphia 12 february 1960	philadelphia orchestra	lp: japanese srokowski society JLSS 1-2 cd: theo van der burg (netherlands)
baltimore 21 february 1962	baltimore symphony	unpublished recording
new york 24 november 1969	american symphony	unpublished recording

l' adorazione dei magi

new york 18 december 1966	american symphony	unpublished recording

SILVESTRE REVUELTAS (1899-1940)

sensemaya

new york 11 december 1947	his symphony orchestra	78: victor 12-0470/18-0169 78: hmv DB 6915 45: victor 49-0882 lp: british stokowski society LS 17 cd: theo van der burg (netherlands) cd: rca/bmg 09026 635482
new york 13 november 1949	new york philharmonic	unpublished recording
philadelphia 17 december 1962	philadelphia orchestra	unpublished recording
new york 3-5 october 1963	american symphony	unpublished recording *rehearsal was apparently also recorded*

GODFREY RIDOUT (1918-1984)

2 mystical songs of john donne

new york 16 october 1953	his symphony orchestra marshall	cd: enno riekena (germany)

WALLINGFORD RIEGGER (1885-1961)

new dance

new york 25 september 1958	his symphony orchestra	cd: cala CACD 0539

passacaglia and fugue

new york 7 october 1968	american symphony	unpublished recording

music for brass choir

illinois 12 november 1952	university symphony	unpublished recording

VITTORIO RIETI (1898-1994)

harpsichord concerto

iew york 26 november .969	american symphony read, harpsichord	unpublished recording

NIKOLAY RIMSKY-KORSAKOV (1844-1908)

scheherazade, symphonic suite

:amden nj march .919	philadelphia orchestra	78: victor 74593/6246 *festival at bagdad only*
amden nj ctober 1920- narch 1921	philadelphia orchestra	78: victor 74691/6246 *young prince and princess only*
hiladelphia nay 927	philadelphia orchestra	cd: biddulph WHL 010 *unpublished victor 78rpm recording of sea and sinbad's ship only*
hiladelphia -13 ctober 927	philadelphia orchestra	78: victor M 23 78: hmv D 1436-1440/D 7692-7696 78: hmv (france) W 968-972 lp: neiman marcus (usa) cd: biddulph WHL 010
hiladelphia 6 march 932	philadelphia orchestra	bell telephone unpublished *rehearsal extracts only*
imden nj october 934	philadelphia orchestra	78: victor M 269 78: hmv DB 2522-2527/DB 7875-7880 cd: nuova era HMT 90017/PH 5001 cd: history 205.652303 cd: cala CACD 0521 cd: andante 2985 *recording completed on 12 november 1934; PH 5001 incorrectly dated 1936*
ndon 3 may 951	philharmonia	lp: hmv ALP 1339 lp: victor LM 1732 lp: british stokowski society LS 12 cd: testament SBT 1129 *recording completed on 14-16 june 1951*
iiladelphia february 962	philadelphia orchestra	lp: grandi concerti GCL 68 cd: frequenz 041.017

new york 17 january 1964	american symphony	unpublished recording *festival at bagdad only*
london 22 september 1964	london symphony	lp: decca LK 4658/PFS 4062 lp: london (usa) PM 55002/SPC 21005 cd: castle classics CCD 102 cd: cala CACD 0536 cd: decca 417 7532/425 8512/475 6090 *cala issue also includes rehearsal extracts*
london 22 december 1964	london symphony	unpublished recording *bbc studio concert*
monte carlo 26 july 1967	monte carlo philharmonic	unpublished recording
london 26 february- 3 march 1975	royal philharmonic	lp: rca ARL1-1182/AGL1-5213/GL 85213 cd: rca/bmg VD 87743/09026 625042/ 09026 684432/82876 658432

dance of the tumblers/the snow maiden

camden nj 19 march 1923	philadelphia orchestra	78: victor 74849/6431 lp: british stokowski society LS 3

flight of the bumble bee/tsar sultan

new york 10 july 1941	all-american symphony	78: columbia (usa) 19005 lp: japanese srokowski society JLSS 4-5 cd: theo van der burg (netherlands)
west ham 12-16 july 1976	national philharmonic	lp: cbs 34543/73589 cd: sony SBK 62647 cd: cala CACD 0529

rimsky-korsakov/**capriccio espagnol**

new york 20 february 1944	nbc symphony	unpublished recording
prague 20 may 1961	czech philharmoic	unpublished video fragment *classical video raritities*
chicago 3 january 1962	chicago symphony	vhs video: video artists international VAI 69603 dvd video: denon (japan) COBO 4061
chicago 14 january 1962	chicago symphony	unpublished recording
new york 21 october 1965	american symphony	unpublished rehearsal recording
new york 26 october 1969	american symphony	unpublished recording
london 11 january 1973	new philharmonia	unpublished recording
london 17-18 january 1973	new philharmonia	lp: decca PFS 4333 lp: london (usa) SPC 21117 cd: decca 417 7532/430 4102/433 6252/ 436 5062/475 6090

christmas eve, suite from the opera

new york 18 december 1965	american symphony	unpublished rehearsal recording
new york 14 december 1969	american symphony	unpublished recording *polonaise only*

le coq d' or, suite from the opera

new york 18-19 january 1970	american symphony	unpublished recording

rimsky-korsakov/**dubinushka**

new york 6 october 1967	american symphony	unpublished recording

ivan the terrible, prelude to act three

philadelphia 9 april 1939	philadelphia orchestra	78: victor M 717 78: hmv DB 6039/DB 6057 cd: biddulph WHL 010 cd: andante 4978
new york 10-12 october 1971	american symphony	cd: theo van der burg (netherlands) *rehearsal was apparently also recorded*
west ham 12-16 july 1976	national philharmonic	lp: cbs 34543/73589

ivan sergeivich, come into the garden/the tsar's bride

los angeles 22 july 1945	hollywood bowl symphony koshetz	cd: eklipse EKRCD 31 cd: enno riekena (germany) cd: bella voce BLV 107.235

the nightingale and the rose

los angeles 22 july 1945	hollywood bowl symphony koshetz	cd: eklipse EKRCD 31 cd: enno riekena (germany) cd: bella voce BLV 107.235

russian easter festival overture

certain of stokowski's recordings of the overture utilise a baritone soloist

philadelphia 26-28 january 1929	philadelphia orchestra	78: victor 7018-7019 78: hmv D 1676-1677 78: hmv (france) W 1043-1044 78: hmv (italy) AW 81and 83 victor L 7002 lp: victor VCM 7101/VIC 6060 lp: rca camden CAL 163 cd: biddulph WHL 010 cd: nuova era HMT 90071/PH 5001 *L 7002 was an experimental 33.1/3 rpm recording (symphonic transcription disc); CAL 163 named performers as warwick symphony otrchestra*
new york 31 march 1942	nbc symphony moscona	unpublished recording

rimsky-korsakov/russian easter festival overture/concluded

new york 23 april 1942	nbc symphony moscona	78: victor M 937 78: hmv DB 6173-6174 cd: cala CACD 0505
new york 6 april 1947	new york philharmonic	unpublished recording
lucerne 11 august 1951	swiss festival orchestra unnamed baritone	cd: relief CR 1882 *opening bars missing from the recording*
san francisco 8-10 december 1952	san francisco symphony rossi-lemeni	cd: archive documents ADCD 200-201 *rehearsal extract*
new york 16 april 1953	his symphony orchestra moscona	lp: victor LM 1816 lp: quintessence PMC 7026 lp: hmv (france) 630215 cd: rediscovery RD 009 cd: theo van der burg (netherlands)
new york 13-18 april 1963	american symphony	unjpublished recording *rehearsal was apparently also recorded*
london 10 september 1966	new philharmonia	unpublished recording
chicago 20-21 february 1968	chicago symphony	lp: victor LSC 3067/VCS 7077 lp: rca SB 6804/GL 42973 cd: rca/bmg GD 60206/09026 604872/ 74321 709312/09026 626042/ 09026 684432/82876 658432
new york 13 april 1968	new york philharmonic	unpublished recording
new york 7 march 1971	american symphony miller	unpublished recording

JOAQUIN RODRIGO (1902-1999)

concierto di aranjuez

new york 16-18 november 1968	american symphony diaz, guitar	unpublished recording *recording incomplete, but rehearsal was apparently also recorded*

BERNARD ROGERS (1893-1968)

fantasy for horn, timpani and strings

new york 25-26 march 1972	american symphony miranda, horn jones, timpani	unpublished recording *rehearsal was apparently also recorded*

NED ROREM (born 1923)

eagles, tone poem

boston 6 march 1964	boston symphony	unpublished recording
tanglewood 21 august 1964	boston symphony	cd: theo van der burg (netherlands)

pilgrims

new york 1 march 1972	american symphony	unpublished recording

DAVID ROSE (1910-1990)

holiday for strings

los angeles 28 july 1946	hollywood bowl symphony	cd: theo van der burg (netherlands)

as kreutzer spins

los angeles 28 july 1946	hollywood bowl symphony	cd: theo van der burg (netherlands)

GIOACHINO ROSSINI (1792-1868)

guilleaume tell. overture

camden nj march 1923	philadelphia orchestra	victor unpublished
west ham march 1976	national philharmonic	lp: pye nixa PCNHX 6 lp: dell' arte DA 9003 lp: vogue CV 25013 cd: pye nixa CDPCN 6 cd: emi CDM 764 1402

guilleaume tell, march

los angeles 26 august 1946	hollywood bowl symphony	lp: japanese srokowski society JLSS 18 cd: theo van der burg (netherlands)

l' italiana in algeri, overture

los angeles 1 september 1946	hollywood bowl symphony	unpublished recording

CLAUDE-JOSEPH ROUGET DE LISLE (1760-1836)

la marseillaise/french national hymn

philadelphia 27 october 1935	philadelphia orchestra	cd: cala CACD 0502 *unpublished victor 78rpm recording*

MIKLOS ROZSA (1907-1995)

pastorale

los angeles 29 july 1945	hollywood bowl symphony	unpublished recording

CARL RUGGLES (1876-1971)

sun-treader

new york 3 december 1967	american symphony	unpublished recording

organum

munich 16 july 1951	bavarian radio symphony	unpublished recording

HARALD SAEVERUD (1897-1992)

ballad of revolt

bergen june 1953	bergen symphony	unpublished recording

CAMILLE SAINT-SAENS (1835-1921)

samson et dalila, scenes from the opera

new york 7 september 1954	nbc symphony shaw chorale stevens peerce merrill	45: victor WDM 1848/ERB 49 lp: victor LM 1848 lp: hmv ALP 1308 lp: british stokowski society LS 15 cd: cala CACD 0540 *recording completed on 14 september 1954; LM 1848 and ALP 1308 omitted one of the recorded scenes (la victoire facile)*

bacchanale/samson et dalila

camden nj 6 january 1920	philadelphia orchestra	78: victor 74671/6241 78: hmv DB 384
philadelphia 13 november 1927	philadelphia orchestra	78: victor 6823 78: hmv D 1807 78: hmv (italy) AW 160 lp: victor VCM 7101 cd: biddulph WHL 012 cd: magic talent MT 48002 cd: grammofono AB 78586 cd: phonographe PH 5025-5026 cd: history 20.3290
los angeles 18 august 1946	hollywood bowl symphony	unpublished recording

le déluge, prelude

los angeles 12 august 1945	hollywood bowl symphony	cd: enno riekena (germany)

saint-saens/**le carnaval des animaux**

philadelphia 26-27 september 1929	philadelphia orchestra barabini and montgomery, pianos	78: victor M 71 78: hmv D 1992-1994/D 7417-7419 78: hmv (france) W 1184-1186 cd: biddulph WHL 012 cd: andante 2985
philadelphia 27 november 1939	philadelphia orchestra levin and behrend, pianos	78: victor M 785 78: hmv DB 5942-5944/DB 8897-8899 78: hmv (australia) ED 247-249 lp: victor VCM 7101 lp: rca camden CAL 100 cd: avid AMSC 601 *side three of the original 78rpm recording was re-made in 1941 without the participation of stokowski; CAL 100 named performers as warwick symphony orchestra*

danse macabre

camden nj march 1923	philadelphia orchestra	victor unpublished
philadelphia 29 april 1925	philadelphia orchestra	78: victor 6505 78: hmv D 1121 78: hmv (france) W 983 78: hmv (italy) AW 4182 78: electrola EJ 49 lp: neiman marcus (usa) cd: biddulph BID 83072 *this was the first electrical recording to be made with a full symphony orchestra*
philadelphia 15 january 1936	philadelphia orchestra	78: victor 14162 78: hmv DB 3077 lp: victor VCM 7101/VIC 6060 lp: rca camden CAL 254 cd: grammofono AB 78552 cd: biddulph WHL 012 cd: magic talent MT 48002 cd: magic master MM 37022 cd: phonographe PH 5025-5026 cd: history 20.3290 *CAL 254 named performers as warwick symphony orchestra; AB 78552 was incorrectly dated 1928*
west ham november 1975	national philharmonic	lp: pye nixa PCNHX 4 lp: vogue CV 25013 cd: pye nixa CDCPN 4 cd: emi CDM 764 4022

ERIK SATIE (1866-1925)

gymnopédie no 1

philadelphia 12 december 1937	philadelphia orchestra	78: victor 1965 78: hmv DA 1688 lp: american stokowski society LSSA 3 cd: biddulph WHL 011 cd: magic talent MT 48015 cd: magic masters MM 37022 cd: history 20.3290 cd: cantus classics 500.090
new york 9 november 1964	american symphony	unpublished rehearsal recording

gymnopédie no 3

philadelphia 12 december 1937	philadelphia orchestra	78: victor 1965 78: hmv DA 1688 lp: american stokowski society LSSA 3 cd: biddulph WHL 011 cd: magic talent MT 48015 cd: magic masters MM 37022 cd: history 20.3290 cd: cantus classics 500.090
new york 9 november 1964	american symphony	unpublished rehearsal recording
new york 1 november 1970	american symphony	unpublished recording

AHMED ADNAN SAYGUN (1907-1991)

yunus emre, oratorio

new york 25 november 1958	symphony of the air and choruses harsonzi wolf wainner gibson	lp: turkish tourist office RW 3967-3968

WALTER SCHARF (born 1910)

palestine suite

los angeles 19 august 1945	hollywood bowl symphony	unpublished recording

ARNOLD SCHOENBERG (1874-1951)

piano concerto

new york 6 february 1944	nbc symphony steuermann, piano	unpublished recording *this was the world premiere performance of the concerto*

friede auf erden

new york 17 december 1967	american symphony orchestra and chorus	unpublished recording

verklärte nacht

new york 3 september 1952	his symphony orchestra	45: victor WDM 1739 lp: victor LM 1739/LM 2117 lp: hmv ALP 1205
new york 23-24 august 1957	his symphony orchestra	lp: capitol P 8433/SP 8433 lp: angel seraphim 60080 cd: emi CDC 747 5212
new york 17-18 november 1960	symphony of the air	cd: library of congress CLC 2 cd: bridge 9074

song of the wood dove/gurrelieder

new york 30 october 1949	new york philharmonic lipton	lp: japanese stokowski society JLSS 99
new york 28 november 1949	new york philharmonic lipton	lp: columbia (usa) ML 2140 cd: cala CACD 0534

schoenberg/**gurrelieder**

philadelphia 8 april 1932	philadelphia orchestra and choruses vreeland bampton althouse betts robofsky de loache	victor unpublished
philadelphia 9 april 1932	philadelphia orchestra and choruses vreeland bampton althouse betts robofsky de loache	LM 127 cd: pearl GEMMCDS 9066 *LM 127 was an experimental 33.1/3 tpm issue (symphonic transcription disc); both issues also included stokowski's spoken outline of themes*
philadelphia 11 april 1932	philadelphia orchestra and choruses vreeland bampton althouse betts robofsky de loache	78: victor M 127 78: hmv DB 1769-1782 lp: victor LCT 6012/AVM2-2017 cd: nuova era HMT 90025-90026 cd: andante 4978 *excerpts* cd: magic talent MT 48015 cd: cantus classics 500.090 *78rpm issues also included stokowski's spoken outline of themes; andante edition includes alternative unpublished takes*
philadelphia 10 march 1961	philadelphia orchestra and choruses rankin zambrana petrak hoffman hagemann	cd: theo van der burg (netherlands)
edinburgh 20 august 1961	london symphony and choruses rankin brouwenstijn mccracken lanigan robinson lidell	cd: theo van der burg (netherlands)

FRANZ SCHUBERT (1797-1828)
symphony no 8 "unfinished"

camden nj december 1923- january 1924	philadelphia orchestra	victor unpublished
camden nj 18 april 1924	philadelphia orchestra	78: victor 74894-74899/6459-6461 78: hmv D 792-794 *stokowski's first published recording of a complete symphonic work*
philadelphia 28-30 april 1928	philadelphia orchestra	78: victor M 16 78: hmv D 1779-1781 78: hmv (france) W 1128-1130 78: electrola EJ 710-712 L 11645-11646 lp: parnassus 5 lp: neiman marcus (usa) cd: biddulph WHL 033 cd: history 205.652303 *L 11645-11646 was an experimental 33.1/3 rpm issue (symphonic transcription disc)*
new york july 1941	all-american symphony	78: columbia (usa) M 485 cd: cala CACD 0520
new york 6 february 1944	nbc symphony	unpublished recording
new york 27 november 1949	new york philharmonic	unpublished recording
boston 12 march 1965	boston symphony	unpublished recording
tanglewood 15 august 1965	boston symphony	cd: theo van der burg (netherlands)
new york 30 january- 3 february 1968	american symphony	unpublished video recording *this was a rehearsal performance*

schubert/symphony no 8/concluded

croydon 8 september 1969	london philharmonic	dvd video: emi classic archive DVA 492 8429
walthamstow 9-10 september 1969	london philharmonic	lp: decca PFS 4197/D 94 D2 lp: london (usa) SPC 21042 cd: decca 475 6090
london 30 september 1973	royal philharmonic	unpublished recording

rosamunde, overture

new york 10 september 1952	his symphony orchestra	lp: victor LM 1730 lp: hmv ALP 1193 lp: british stokowski society LS 18 cd: rediscovery RD 76 cd: otaken (japan)
west ham march 1976	national philharmonic	lp: pye nixa PCNHX 6 lp: dell' arte DA 9003 lp: vogue CV 25013 cd: pye nixa CDPCN 6 cd: emi CDM 764 1402

rosamunde, entr' acte no 3

new york 10 september 1952	his symphony orchestra	lp: victor LM 1730 lp: hmv ALP 1193 lp: british stokowski society LS 18 cd: rediscovery RD 76 cd: otaken (japan) cd: theo van der burg (netherlands)

schubert/**rosamunde, ballet music no 2**

philadelphia 2 may 1927	philadelphia orchestra	cd: biddulph WHL 033 *unpublished victor 78rpm recording*
philadelphia 11 october 1927	philadelphia orchestra	78: victor 1312 lp: rca camden CAL 123 cd: biddulph WHL 033 *CAL 123 named performers as warwick symphony orchestra*
philadelphia 4 december 1931	philadelphia orchestra	bell telephone unpublished
new york 10 september 1952	his symphony orchestra	lp: victor LM 1730 lp: hmv ALP 1193 lp: british stokowski society LS 18 cd: rediscovery RD 76 cd: otaken (japan) cd: theo van der burg (netherlands)
new york 9 november 1963	american symphony	unpublished rehearsal recording

tyrolean dances/german dances d783

camden nj october- november 1922	philadelphia orchestra	victor unpublished *dance no 3 only*
camden nj 12 december 1922	philadelphia orchestra	78: victor 74814 *dance no 3 only*
new york 10 december 1944	new york city symphony	cd: cala CACD 0502 cd: magic master MM 37031 cd: cantus classics 500.090 *unpublished victor 78rpm recording*
new york 10 june 1949	his symphony orchestra	78: victor 10-1519 45: victor 49-0814/ERA 67 45: hmv 7ER 5043 lp: victor LM 1238 lp: british stokowski society LS 18 cd: theo van der burg (netherlands)

schubert/**marche militaire**

los angeles 2 september 1945	hollywood bowl symphony	lp: kensington (usa) M 1030

moment musical no 3

camden nj 27 january 1922	philadelphia orchestra	78: victor 66098/799
philadelphia 6 april 1927	philadelphia orchestra	78: victor 1312 45: rca camden CAE 188 lp: rca camden CAL 123 lp: neiman marcus (usa) cd: biddulph WHL 033 *CAE 188 and CAL 123 named performers as warwick symphony orchestra*
los angeles july 1945	hollywood bowl symphony	78: victor 11-9174/M 1062 78: hmv DB 10130
los angeles 19 august 1945	hollywood bowl symphony	unpublished recording
new york 6-11 october 1970	american symphony	lp: japanese srokowski society JLSS 23-24
london 15 june 1972	london symphony	lp: decca PFS 4351 lp: london (usa) SPC 21130 cd: pickwick IMPX 9033 cd: decca 433 8762/448 9462/475 1452

schubert/**ave maria**		
philadelphia april 1939	philadelphia orchestra novis	*fantasia soundtrack recording* lp: top rank 30-003 lp: disneyland WDL 4101/ST 3926/STER 101 lp: buena vista BVS 101 cd: buena vista CD 020/60007 cd: pony canyon PCCD 00009 cd: avex AVCW 12048-12049/12163-12164 cd: pickwick DSTCD 452 vhs video: buena vista D 211322 vhs video: disneyland 101 dvd video: disney classics ZIDD 888113/888 055
new york 1944	orchestra anderson	unpublished video recording *this television recording is referred to by enno riekena but no further confirmation of details could be found*
ständchen		
philadelphia 27 october 1935	philadelphia orchestra	cd: cala CACD 0502 *unpublished victor 78rpm recording*

WILLIAM SCHUMAN (1910-1992)

symphony no 7		
new york 9 november 1964	american symphony	unpublished rehearsal recording
prayer in time of war		
new york 12 december 1943	nbc symphony	unpublished recording

ROBERT SCHUMANN (1810-1856)

symphony no 2

philadelphia 4-5 december 1931	philadelphia orchestra	bell telephone unpublished
new york 6 february 1949	new york philharmonic	unpublished recording
new york 18-21 july 1950	his symphony orchestra	45: victor WDM 1614 lp: victor LM 1194 lp: british stokowski sociery LS 8 cd: theo van der burg (netherlands) cd: cala CACD 0532
new york 18 april 1966	american symphony	unpublished recording
new york 6-11 october 1970	american symphony	unpublished recording

symphony no 4

montreux 11 september 1968	orchestre de la suisse romande	lp: japanese stokowski society JLSS 22 cd: theo van der burg (netherlands)

piano concerto

los angeles 1 september 1946	hollywood bowl symphony eustis, piano	unpublished recording *first movement only performed at this concert*

cello concerto

new york 6 november 1949	new york philharmonic fournier, cello	cd: arlecchino ARL 169 cd: theo van der burg (netherlands)

träumerei

new york 11 july 1941	all-american symphony	78: columbia (usa) 11982 lp: american stokowski society LSSA 6 cd: theo van der burg (netherlands)

CYRIL SCOTT (1879-1970)

hornpipe and shanty

los angeles 21 july 1946	hollywood bowl symphony	cd: enno riekena (germany)

THOMAS SCOTT (1912-1961)

from the sacred harp

new york 30 january 1949	new york philharmonic	v-disc 896 cd: wing (japan) WCD 39 cd: cala CACD 0537

ALEXANDER SCRIABIN (1872-1915)

poeme de l' extase

philadelphia 16 march 1932	philadelphia orchestra	bell telephone unpublished *these were rehearsal extracts*
camden nj 19 march 1932	philadelphia orchestra	78: victor M 125 78: hmv DB 1706-1707 L 11616-11617 cd: pearl GEMMCD 9066 cd: andante 2985 *L 11616-11617 was an experimental 33.1/3 rpm issue (symphonic transcription disc)*
houston 19 march 1958	houston symphony	lp: everest LPBR 6032/SDBR 3032 lp: concert hall SMSC 2533 cd: philips (usa) 422 3062 cd: panthéon D 1032X cd: everest EVC 9037
london 18 june 1968	new philharmonia	cd: bbc legends BBCL 40182
london 15 june 1969	royal philharmonic	cd: music and arts CD 847 cd: bbc legends BBCL 40692
prague 7-8 september 1972	czech philharmonic	lp: decca PFS 4333/D94 D2 lp: london (usa) SPC 21117/SPC 21136 cd: decca 443 8982/475 1452

scriabin/**poeme du feu**

philadelphia 12 march 1932	philadelphia orchestra curtis institute choir levin, piano	lp: bell telephone laboratories BTL 7901 cd: iron needle IN 1402 cd: history 20.3290 *these were rehearsal extracts*
camden nj 19 march 1932	philadelphia orchestra curtis institute choir levin, piano	78: victor M 125 78: victor DB 1708-1709 L 11616-11617 cd: pearl GEMMCD 9066 cd: andante 2985 *L 11616-11617 was an experimental 33.1/3 rpm issue (symphonic transcription disc)*

étude in c sharp minor

new york 11 december 1944	new york city symphony	cd: cala CACD 0502 cd: magic master MM 37031 cd: cantus classics 500.090 cd: history 20.3290 *unpublished victor 78rpm recording*
los angeles 26 august 1945	hollywood bowl symphony	cd: enno riekena (germany)
new york 8 may 1970	american symphony	unpublished recording
new york 26 april 1971	american symphony	lp: vanguard VCS 10095/VSQ 30001 cd: vanguard OVC 8012/08.616271
new york 27 april 1971	american symphony	unpublished recording
london 15 june 1972	london symphony	unpublished recording

JOSE SEREBRIER (born 1938)

poema elegiaco

new york 3-5 october 1963	american symphony	unpublished recording

MINAO SHIBATA (1916-1996)

sinfonia

tokyo 8 july 1965	japan philharmonic	unpublished recording

NATHANIEL SHILKRET (1889-1982)

trombone concerto

new york 15 february 1945	new york city symphony dorsey, trombone	unpublished recording

DMITRI SHOSTAKOVICH (1906-1975)

symphony no 1

camden nj 18 november 1933	philadelphia orchestra	78: victor M 192 78: hmv DB 2203-2207/DB 3847-3851 LM 192 cd: pearl GEMMCD 9044 *LM 192 was an experimental 33.1/3 rpm issue (symphonic transcription disc)*
los angeles 23 july 1946	hollywood bowl symphony	unpublished recording
new york 18 december 1958	symphony of the air	lp: united artists UAL 7004/UAS 8004 cd: emi CMS 565 4272/566 8642
new york 5 march 1960	new york philharmonic	unpublished recording
new york 21-23 december 1968	american symphony	unpublished recording *rehearsal was apparently also recorded*

shostakovich/**symphony no 5**

philadelphia 20 april 1939	philadelphia orchestra	78: victor M 619 78: hmv DB 3991-3996/DB 8933-8938 lp: american stokowski society LSSA 4 cd: pearl GEMMCDS 9044 cd: dutton CDAX 8017 cd: history 205.652303
new york 1 october 1958	new york philharmonic	lp: everst LPBR 6010/SDBR 3010 lp: world records T 281/ST 281 lp: concert hall SMS 2830 cd: priceless D 22697 cd: philips (usa) 422 3062 cd: everest EVC 9030 *orchestra described for this recording as stadium symphony orchestra*
leipzig 1 june 1959	gewandhaus orchestra	unpublished recording
london 30 june 1959	london symphony	unpublished recording
philadelphia 12 february 1960	philadelphia orchestra	lp: japanese stokowski society JLSS 1-2 cd: theo van der burg (netherlands)
houston 7 november 1960	houston symphony	unpublished recording
prague 20 may 1961	czech philharmonic	cd: preludio PR 2156
edinburgh 22 august 1961	london symphony	unpublished recording
new york 2 march 1962	new york philharmonic	unpublished recording

shostakovich/symphony no 5/concluded

new york 21 december 1963	american symphony	unpublished rehearsal recording
philadelphia 4 february 1964	philadelphia orchestra	unpublished recording
london 17 september 1964	london symphony	cd: music and arts CD 765 cd: bbc radio classics 15656 91542 cd: bbc legends BBCL 41652
boston 12 march 1965	boston symphony	unpublished recording
tanglewood 15 august 1965	boston symphony	cd: theo van der burg (netherlands)
new york 7-9 may 1972	american symphony	unpublished recording

symphony no 6

philadelphia 29 november 1940	philadelphia orchestra	unpublished recording
philadelphia 8 december 1940	philadelphia orchestra	78: victor M 867 cd: dell' arte DA 9023 cd: dutton CDAX 8017 *recording completed on 28 december 1940*
chicago 21 february 1968	chicago symphony	lp: victor LSC 3133/AGL1-5063 lp: rca SB 6839 cd: rca/bmg 09026 625162/09026 684432
new york 13 april 1968	new york philharmonic	unpublished recording

shostakovich/**symphony no 7 "leningrad"**

new york 13 december 1942	nbc symphony	cd: pearl GEMMCDS 9044 cd: theo van der burg (netherlands)

symphony no 8

new york february 1945	new york city symphony	unpublished recording

symphony no 10

new york 16 january 1965	american symphony	unpublished rehearsal recording
philadelphia 21 june 1965	philadelphia orchestra	unpublished recording *scherzo movement only performed at this concert*
chicago 24 march 1966	chicago symphony	lp: japanese stokowski society JLSS 21 cd: chicago symphony orchestra CSO 90/12

symphony no 11 "the year 1905"

houston 9-12 april 1958	houston symphony	lp: capitol PBR 8448/SPBO 8700 lp: angel seraphim 60228 lp: everest SDBR 3310 lp: world records T 776-777/ST 776-777 lp: angel 34446 cd: emi CDC 747 4192/CDM 565 2062
moscow 7 june 1958	ussr large radio symphony	cd: russian disc RDCD 15100

the age of gold, suite from the ballet

chicago 15-21 february 1968	chicago symphony	lp: victor LSC 3133/AGL1-5063 lp: rca SB 6839 cd: rca/bmg 74321 769312/09026 625162/ 09026 684432 *polka only* lp: victor VCS 7077

lady macbeth of mzensk, entr' acte

new york 18 december 1958	symphony of the air	lp: united artists UAL 7004/UAS 8004 cd: emi CMS 565 4272

shostakovich/**prelude in e flat minor**

camden nj 30 december 1935	philadelphia orchestra	78: victor M 192/M 291 78: hmv DB 2884 lp: american stokowski society LSSA 4 cd: pearl GEMMCDS 9044 cd: dutton CDAX 8002
new york 14 november 1940	all-american symphony	78: columbia (usa) 12903/M 446 cd: andante 2985
new york 30 january 1944	nbc symphony	unpublished recording
los angeles 22 july 1945	hollywood bowl symphony	cd: enno riekena (germany)
new york 19 october 1947	new york philharmonic	lp: japanese stokowski society JLSS 9 cd: theo van der burg (netherlands)
scheveningen 27 june 1951	residentie orchestra	cd: residentie orchestra anniversary album cd: theo van der burg (netherlands)
chicago 9 january 1958	chicago symphony	unpublished recording
new york 18 december 1958	symphony of the air	lp: united artists UAL 7004/UAS 8004 cd: emi CMS 565 4272
london 15 june 1969	royal philharmonic	cd: music and arts CD 847 cd: bbc legends BBCL 40692
new york 6 april 1971	american symphony	unpublished recording
west ham july 1976	national philharmonic	lp: cbs 34543/73589 cd: cala CACD 0529

JEAN SIBELIUS (1865-1957)

symphony no 1

new york 11-13 july 1950	his symphony orchestra	78: victor M 1497 78: hmv DB 21264-21267 45: victor WDM 1497 lp: victor LM 1125 lp: hmv ALP 1210 lp: british stokowski society LS 16 cd: theo van der burg (netherlands) cd: rediscovery RD 76 cd: cala CACD 0541
helsinki 17 june 1953	helsinki city symphony	cd: enno riekena (germany)
west ham 2-5 november 1976	national philharmonic	lp: cbs 34548/76666 cd: sony SBK2 63260 cd: emi 575 4812

symphony no 2

new york 15-16 september 1954	nbc symphony	lp: victor LM 1854 lp: hmv ALP 1440 lp: dell' arte DA 9002 cd: theo van der burg (netherlands) cd: cala CACD 0541
new york 21 january 1964	american symphony	unpublished rehearsal recording
london 15 september 1964	bbc symphony	cd: bbc legends BBCL 41152
philadelphia 18 december 1964	philadelphia orchestra	cd: philadelphia orchestra POA 100

sibelius/**symphony no 4**

camden nj 23 april 1932	philadelphia orchestra	78: victor M 160 L 11638-11639 lp: victor SRS 3001 cd: dell' arte DA 9023 cd: biddulph WHL 062 cd: history 205.652303 *L 11638-11639 was an experimental 33.1/3 rpm issue (symphonic transcription disc)*
philadelphia 16 march 1962	philadelphia orchestra	unpublished recording

symphony no 7

new york 22 september 1940	all-american symphony	lp: american stokowski society LSSA 6 cd: music and arts CD 841 *unpublished columbia 78rpm recording*
helsinki 17 june 1953	helsinki city symphony	cd: enno riekena (germany)

violin concerto

camden nj december 1934	philadelphia orchestra heifetz, violin	cd: philadelphia orchestra POA 100 *unpublished victor 78rpm recording*
new york 1-3 november 1970	american symphony szeryng, violin	cd: venezia (japan) V 1004

pelleas and melisande, movements from the incidental music

helsinki 17 june 1953	helsinki city symphony	cd: enno riekena (germany)

girl with roses/swan white

new york 17 november 1947	new york philharmonic	78: columbia (usa) M 80 cd: cala CACD 0534

sibelius/**berceuse/the tempest**

philadelphia 7 november 1937	philadelphia orchestra	78: victor 14726 78: hmv DB 3534/DB 6009 45: rca camden CAE 188 lp: tca camden CAL 123 cd: dell' arte DA 9023 cd: biddulph WHL 062 *biddulph issue is dated 15 january 1936; CAE 188 and CAL 123 named performers as warwick symphony orchestra*
new york 4 october 1949	his symphony orchestra	78: victor 12-1191 78: hmv DB 21334 45: victor 49-1168 45: hmv 7R 101 45: hmv (italy) 7RQ 180 45: electrola 7RW 137 lp: victor LM 1238/LRM 7024 lp: british stokowski society LS 16 cd: theo van der burg (netherlands) cd: cala CACD 0542

valse triste

philadelphia 15 january 1936	philadelphia orchestra	78: victor 14726 78: hmv DB 3318/DB 6009 45: rca camden CAE 188 lp: rca camden CAL 123 cd: dell' arte DA 9023 cd: andante 2985 *CAE 188 and CAL 123 named performers as warwick symphony orchestra*
new york 4 october 1949	his symphony orchestra	78: victor 12-1191 78: hmv DB 21334 45: victor 49-1168 45: hmv 7R 101 45: hmv (italy) 7RQ 180 45: electrola 7RW 137 lp: victor LM 1238/LRM 7024 lp: british stokowski society LS 16 cd: theo van der burg (netherlands) cd: cala CACD 0542

sibelius/**the swan of tuonela**

philadelphia may 1929	philadelphia orchestra	78: victor 7380 78: hmv D 1997 78: hmv (france) W 1188 78: hmv (italy) AW 267 L 11656 lp: victor VCM 7101 cd: biddulph WHL 047 cd: grammofono AB 78586 cd: magic talent MT 48015 cd: phonographe PH 5025-5026 cd: cantus classics 500.090 cd: history 20.3290 cd: andante 2985 *L 11656 was an experimental 33.1/3 rpm issue (symphonic transcription disc)*
philadelphia 8 december 1935	philadelphia orchestra	unpublished recording
los angeles 28 july 1946	hollywood bowl symphony	unpublished recording
new york 11 december 1947	his symphony orchestra	78: victor 12-0585 78: hmv DB 21555 45: victor 49-0461 lp: victor LM 9029/LM 151/LRM 7024 lp: british stokowski society LS 16 cd: cala CACD 0522
new york 5 may 1957	his symphony orchestra	45: capitol FAP 48399/SFP 48399 lp: capitol P 8399/P 8673/SP 8399/ SP 8673 lp: angel seraphim 6094 lp: emi SMFP 2145 cd: emi CDM 565 6142 *recording completed on 15 may 1957*
new york 24 april 1965	american symphony	unpublished rehearsal recording
cleveland 13 february 1971	cleveland orchestra	unpublished recording
west ham 2-5 november 1976	national philharmonic	lp: cbs 34548/76666 cd: sony SBK2 63260

camden nj 18 march 1921	philadelphia orchestra	78: victor 74698/6366 78: hmv DB 599 *this was an abridged version of the work*
camden nj 28 april 1930	philadelphia orchestra	78: victor 7412 78: hmv DB 1584 L 11656 45: rca camden CAE 101 lp: victor VCM 7101 lp: rca camden CAL 120 cd: biddulph WHL 047 cd: magic talent MT 48015 cd: phonographe PH 5025-5026 cd: cantus classics 500.090 cd: history 20.3290 *L 11656 was an experimental 33/1/3 rpm issue (symphonic transcription disc); CAE 101 and CAL 120 named performers as warwick symphony orchestra*
helsinki 17 june 1953	helsinki city symphony	cd: enno riekena (germany)
new york 5 may 1957	his symphony orchestra	45: capitol FAP 48399/SFP 48399 lp: capitol P 8399/SP 8399 lp: angel seraphim 6094 lp: emi SMFP 2145 cd: emi CDM 565 6142 *recording completed on 15 may 1957*

ELLIE SIEGMEISTER (1909-1991)

symphony no 1

new york 2 november 1947	new york philharmonic	unpublished recording

western suite

los angeles 28 july 1946	hollywood bowl symphony	cd: theo van der burg (netherlands)

harvest evening

new york 29 december 1946	new york philharmonic	unpublished recording

CHARLES SANFORD SKILTON (1868-1941)

sunrise song

new york 16 january 1944	nbc symphony	unpublished recording

BEDRICH SMETANA (1824-1884)

the moldau/ma vlast

new york 18 february 1960	rca victor symphony	lp: victor LM 2471/LSC 2471/VCS 7077/ AGL1-5259 lp: rca RB 16259/SB 2130 cd: rca/bmg 09026 615032/09026 626012/ 09026 684443/74321 709312

sarka/ma vlast

philadelphia 18 december 1964	philadelphia orchestra	unpublished recording

the bartered bride, overture

new york 18 february 1960	rca victor symphony	lp: victor LM 2471/LSC 2471/VCS 7077/ AGL1-5259 lp: rca RB 16259/SB 2130 cd: rca/bmg 09026 615032/09026 626012/ 09026 684443

JOHN PHILIP SOUSA (1854-1932)

el capitan, march

camden nj 15 march 1930	philadelphia orchestra	78: victor 1441 78: hmv E 556 lp: japanese stokowski society JLSS 23-24 cd: japanese stokowski society LSCD 20 cd: cala CACD 0501 cd: music and arts CD 1173 *cd editions contain different takes of the 78rpm recording*

manhattan beach, march

philadelphia 27 september 1929	philadelphia orchestra	cd: japanese stokowski society LSCD 20 *unpublished victor 78rpm recording*

stars and stripes forever, march

philadelphia 27 september 1929	philadelphia orchestra	78: victor 1441 78: hmv E 556 lp: japanese stokowski society JLSS 23-24 cd: japanese stokowski society LSCD 20 cd: music and arts CD 1173
new york 9 november 1963	american symphony	lp: japanese stokowski society JLSS 23-24 *this was a rehearsal extract*
tokyo 13 july 1965	japan philharmonic	unpublished recording
west ham november 1975	national philharmonic	45: nimbus 45204 lp: pye nixa PCNHX 4 cd: emi CDM 764 1402

JOHN STAFFORD SMITH (1750-1836)

the star-spangled banner/american national hymn

new york july 1940	all-american symphony	78: columbia (usa) 17204
new york 4 november 1941	nbc symphony	unpublished recording
new york 11 november 1941	nbc symphony	unpublished recording
new york 18 november 1941	nbc symphony	unpublished recording
new york 25 november 1941	nbc symphony	unpublished recording
new york 24 march 1942	nbc symphony	unpublished recording
new york 16 april 1966	metropolitan opera orchestra	lp: mrf records MRF 7 *final performance in the old metropolitan opera house*
new york 10 october 1966	american symphony	lp: japanese stokowski society JLSS 22 cd: theo van der burg (netherlands)
philadelphia 14 october 1966	philadelphia orchestra	unpublished recording
new york 12 december 1966	american symphony schola cantorum	unpublished recording
new york 7 may 1967	american symphony	unpublished recording

ALEXANDER STEINERT (1900-1982)

rhapsody for clarinet and orchestra

los angeles 12 august 1945	hollywood bowl symphony bloch, clarinet	cd: enno riekena (germany)

HALSEY STEVENS (1908-1989)

symphony no 2

new york 22 february 1953	cbs studio orchestra	cd: enno riekena (germany)

WILLIAM GRANT STILL (1895-1978)

scherzo/afro-american symphony

new york 13 november 1940	all american symphony	78: columbia (usa) 11992 lp: american stokowski society LSSA 6 cd: theo van der burg (netherlands)

festive overture

new york 6 april 1947	new york philharmonic	unpublished recording

and they lynched him on a tree

new york 14 april 1942	nbc symphony collegiate choir	unpublished recording

EDGAR STILLMAN-KELLEY (1867-1944)

alice in wonderland, suite

camden nj december 1924	philadelphia orchestra	victor unpublished

LEOPOLD STOKOWSKI (1882-1977)

balance test march

philadelphia 2 may 1927	philadelphia orchestra	cd: cala CACD 0502 *unpublished victor 78rpm recording*

reveries

new york 1 march 1972	american symphony	lp: japanese stokowski society JLSS 23-24

when christ was born

new york 29 december 1971	saint patrick's choir dunner, organ	unpublished recording

JOHANN STRAUSS II (1825-1899)

du und du, waltz

los angeles 12 august 1945	hollywood bowl symphony	cd: enno riekena (germany)
los angeles 28 july 1946	hollywood bowl symphony	unpublished rcording
los angeles 23 august 1946	hollywood bowl symphony	78: victor 10-1310 45: victor 49-0279/ERA 67
los angeles 26 august 1946	hollywood bowl symphony	lp: japanese stokowski society JLSS 18 cd: theo van der burg (netherlands)

pizzicato polka

philadelphia 21 june 1965	philadelphia orchestra	unpublished recording

j.strauss/an der schönen blauen donau, waltz

camden nj 10 may 1919	philadelphia orchestra	78: victor 74627/6237
philadelphia 10 june 1926	philadelphia orchestra	78: victor 6584 78: hmv D 1218
philadelphia 9 april 1939	philadelphia orchestra	78: victor 15425 78: hmv DB 3821 lp: victor LM 6074 cd: music and arts CD 1173
new york 22 september 1949	his symphony orchestra	78: victor 12-1160 78: hmv DB 21346 45: victor 49-1076/WDM 1438 45: hmv 7R 169 45: hmv (italy) 7RQ 182 cd: theo van der burg (netherlands) cd: cala CACD 0532
new york 23 october 1949	new york philharmonic	lp: japanese stokowski society JLSS 09 cd: theo van der burg (netherlands)
new york january- february 1955	nbc symphony	45: victor ERA 259 lp: victor LM 2042 lp: japanese stokowski society JLSS 17 cd: cala CACD 0543 *unpublished stereophonic edition of this recording may also survive*
new york february 1957	his symphony orchestra	lp: capitol P 8399/P 8694/SP 8399/ SP 8694 lp: angel seraphim 6094 lp: emi SMFP 2145

j.strauss/**g'schichten aus dem wienerwald, waltz**

camden nj may 1920	philadelphia orchestra	victor unpublished
philadelphia 10 june 1926	philadelphia orchestra	78: victor 6584 78: hmv D 1218
philadelphia 9 april 1939	philadelphia orchestra	78: victor 15425 78: hmv DB 3821 lp: victor LM 6074 lp: rca camden CAL 153/CFL 103 cd: music and arts CD 1173 *CAL 153 named performers as warwick symphony orchestra*
new york 22 september 1949	new york philharmonic	78: victor 12-1160 78: hmv DB 21346 45: victor 49-1076 45: hmv 7R 169 45: hmv (italy) 7RQ 182 cd: cala CACD 0532
new york january- february 1955	nbc symphony	45: victor ERA 259 lp: victor LM 2042 cd: cala CACD 0543 *unpublished stereophonic edition of this recording may also survive*
west ham november 1975	national philharmonic	lp: pye nixa PCNHX 4 cd: pye nixa CDPCN 4

RICHARD STRAUSS (1864-1949)

also sprach zarathustra

new york 15-17 november 1970	american symphony	unpublished recording *rehearsal was apparently also recorded*

don juan

new york 12 october 1958	new york philharmonic	lp: everest LPBR 6023/SDBR 3023 lp: world records T 108/ST 108/PE 751 lp: sine qua non SQN 7115 lp: concert hall SMS 2832 cd: priceless D 1323X cd: bescol CD 538 cd: virtuoso 3602 cd: everest EVC 9004 *orchestra described for this recording as stadium symphony*

strauss/gavotte from the suite for wind instruments

new york 22 january 1957	his symphony orchestra	lp: capitol P 8385/SP 8385 cd: emi CDM 565 6142 *recording completed on 29 january 1957*

metamorphosen

new york 19 march 1947	columbia symphony	lp: japanese stokowski society JLSS 15

der rosenkavalier, suite from the opera

los angeles 26 august 1945	hollywood bowl symphony	cd: enno riekena (germany)
new york 23 march 1971	american symphony	unpublished recording

dance of the 7 veils/salome

camden nj 5 december 1921	philadelphia orchestra	78: victor 74729-74730/6240 78: hmv DB 383
philadelphia 1 may 1929	philadelphia orchestra	78: victor 7259-7260 78: hmv D 1935-1936 78: hmv (italy) AW 207-208 lp: rca camden CAL 254 cd: music and arts CD 1173 *CAL 254 named performers as warwick symphony*
philadelphia 5 april 1937	philadelphia orchestra	cd: cala CACD 0502 cd: magic talent MT 48033 cd: cantus classics 500.090 *unpublished victor 78rpm recording*
new york 1941	all-american symphony	unpublished recording
los angeles 6 august 1946	hollywood bowl symphony	unpublished recording
new york 12 october 1958	new york philharmonic	lp: everest LPBR 6023/SDBR 3023 lp: world records T 108/ST 108/PE 751 lp: concert hall SMS 2832 lp: sine qua non SQN 7115 cd: priceless D 1323X cd: bescol CD 538 cd: everest EVC 9004 *orchestra described for this recording as stadium symphony*
philadelphia 19 january 1963	philadelphia orchestra	cd: bella voce BLV 107.235

strauss/**till eulenspiegels lustige streiche**

new york 12 october 1958	new york philharmonic	lp: everest LPBR 6023/SDBR 3023 lp: world records T 108/ST 108/PR 751 lp: concert hall SMS 2832 lp: sine qua non SQN 7715 cd: priceless D 1323X cd: bescol CD 538 cd: virtuoso 3602 cd: everest EVC 9004 *orchestra described for this recording as stadium symphony*

tod und verklärung

camden nj 7 april 1934	philadelphia orchestra	78: victor M 217 78: hmv DB 2324-2326 cd: rca/bmg 09026 609292 cd: history 205.652303
new york 3-4 july 1941	all-american symphony	78: columbia (usa) M 492 cd: music and arts CD 845 cd: andante 2985
new york 21 november 1944	new york city symphony	unpublished recording
new york 10 december 1944	new york city symphony	78: victor M 1006 78: hmv DB 6320-6322 lp: rca camden CAL 189 lp: american stokowski society LSSA 5 cd: cala CACD 0506 cd: membran 222174 *CAL 189 named performers as sutton symphony orchestra*
new york 24 january 1964	american symphony	unpublished rehearsal recording
tanglewood 21 august 1964	boston symphony	cd: theo van der burg (netherlands)

IGOR STRAVINSKY (1882-1972)

symphony in c

new york 21 february 1943	nbc symphony	unpublished recording

symphony of psalms

philadelphia 12 march 1932	philadelphia orchestra and chorus	bell telephone unpublished

violin concerto

philadelphia 8 january 1932	philadelphia orchestra dushkin, violin	bell telephone unpublished

concerto for strings

new york 6 april 1948	new york philharmonic	unpublished recording

fireworks

camden nj 6 november 1922	philadelphia orchestra	78: victor 1112 lp: british stokowski society LS 3 cd: pearl GEMMCD 9031 cd: dutton CDAX 8002

circus polka

new york 21 february 1943	nbc symphony	unpublished recording

stravinsky/**l' histoire du soldat**

new york 17-18 november 1966	instrumental ensemble milhaud aumont singher	*complete version in french* lp: vanguard VRS 1165/VSD 71165 lp: world records T 858/ST 858 lp: festival classique FC 442 cd: vanguard VCS 10121/OVC 8004/SVC 1 *also published in sacd format* *complete version in english* lp: vanguard VRS 1166/VSD 71166 cd: vanguard SVC 92 *instrumental sections only* lp: vanguard VSD 707-708 lp: analogue productions APC 031 cd: vanguard OVC 8013

mass

frankfurt 31 may 1955	hessischer rundfunk orchestra and chorus soloists	unpublished recording
new york 14 december 1969	american symphony orchestra and chorus soloists	unpublished recording

pastorale

camden nj 26 november 1934	philadelphia orchestra	78: victor 1998 cd: pearl GEMMCD 9031 cd: dutton CDAX 8002
london 15 june 1969	royal philharmonic	cd: music and arts CD 847 cd: bbc legends BBCL 40692
london 17 june 1969	royal philharmonic	lp: decca PFS 4189/SPA 159 lp: london (usa) SPC 21041 cd: decca 433 8762/443 8982
new york 18-19 january 1970	american symphony	unpublished recording

stravinsky/l' oiseau de feu, suite from the ballet

camden nj october 1924	philadelphia orchestra	victor unpublished
camden nj 13 october 1924	philadelphia orchestra	78: victor 6492-6493 78: hmv DB 841-842 *recording completed on 8 december 1924*
philadelphia 12 october 1927	philadelphia orchestra	78: victor M 53 lp: rca DPM2-0534 lp: dell' arte DA 9005 cd: biddulph WHL 005
camden nj 25 november 1935	philadelphia orchestra	78: victor M 291 78: hmv DB 2882-2884 cd: pearl GEMMCD 9031 cd: dutton CDAX 8002 cd: history 20.3290 *recording completed on 30 december 1935*
new york 14 april 1940	all-american symphony	78: columbia (usa) M 446
new york 7 april 1942	nbc symphony	cd: enno riekena (germany)
new york 27 april 1942	nbc symphony	78: victor M 933 cd: cala CACD 0505
new york 24 may 1950	his symphony orchestra	78: victor M 1421 45: victor WDM 1421 lp: victor LM 44/LM 6113/LM 9029 lp: hmv (italy) QBLP 1020 *recording completed on 7 june 1950*
munich 16 july 1951	bavarian radio orchestra	cd: theo van der burg (netherlands)

stravinsky/l' oiseau de feu ballet suite/concluded

berlin 18-20 may 1957	berlin philharmonic	lp: capitol P 8407/SP 8407 lp: angel seraphim 60229 lp: emi CFP 134/SHZEL 78 cd: emi CDM 769 1162/CDEM 565 2072/ 572 3382
new york 5 october 1963	american symphony	unpublished rehearsal recording
london 15 june 1967	london symphony	unpublished recording
london 16 june 1967	london symphony	lp: decca LK 4927/PFS 4139 lp: london (usa) SPC 21026 lp: musical heritage society MHS 827052 cd: decca 443 8982/475 1452

petrushka, complete ballet

philadelphia 19 april 1937	philadelphia orchestra	78: victor M 574/M 1064 78: hmv DB 3511-3514 lp: rca camden CAL 203 lp: rca DPN2-0534 cd: pearl GEMMCD 9031 cd: dutton CDAX 8002 cd: rca/bmg 09026 613942 cd: history 205.652303 *recording completed on 7 november 1937; CAL 203 named performers as warwick symphony orchestra*
new york 30 june- 5 july 1950	his symphony orchestra	lp: victor LM 1175 lp: hmv ALP 1240 cd: testament SBT 1139

stravinsky/**petrushka, suite from the ballet**

new york 20 february 1944	nbc symphony	unpublished recording
berlin 18-20 may 1957	berlin philharmonic	lp: capitol P 8407/SP 8407 lp: angel seraphim 60229 lp: emi CFP 134/SHZEL 78 cd: emi CDM 769 1162/CDM 565 4232/ 572 3382
philadelphia 17 december 1962	philadelphia orchestra	lp: grandi concerti GCL 57 cd: theo van der burg (netherlands)
baltimore 10 january 1963	baltimore symphony	unpublished recording
boston 6 march 1964	boston symphony	cd: theo van der burg (netherlands)
tanglewood 21 august 1964	boston symphony	cd: theo van der burg (netherlands)
tokyo july 1965	japan philharmonic	cd: plarz (japan) P23G 535 cd: kapelle (japan) 32G 175807 *these were rehearsal extracts*
philadelphia 14 october 1966	philadelphia orchestra	unpublished recording
budapest 2 february 1967	hungarian state symphony	lp: british stokowski society LS 2 cd: theo van der burg (netherlands)
copenhagen 4 august 1967	danish radio orchestra	unpublished recording
philadelphia 13 february 1969	philadelphia orchestra	unpublished recording
new york 23 march 1971	american symphony	unpublished recording

stravinsky/**le sacre du printemps**

philadelphia 24-26 september 1929	philadelphia orchestrra	78: victor M 74 78: hmv D 1919-1922/D 7602-7605 78: electrola EJ 626-629 lp: rca DPM2-0534 lp: dell' arte DA 9005 cd: rca/bmg 09026 613942 cd: pearl GEMMCD 9488 cd: magic talent MT 48002 cd: history 20.3290 cd: documents 221708 *recording completed on 12 march 1930*
philadelphia april 1939	philadelphia orchestra	*fantasia soundtrack recording of abridged version* lp: top rank 30-003 lp: disneyland WDL 4101/ST 3926/STER 101 lp: buena vista BVS 101 cd: buena vista CD 020/60007 cd: pony canyon PCCD 00009 cd: avex AVCW 12048-12049/12163-12164 cd: pickwick DSTCD 452 vhs video: buena vista D 211322 vhs video: disneyland 101 dvd video: disney classics ZIDD 888113/888055
new york 30 january 1965	american symphony	unpublished rehearsal recording

LAMAR STRINGFIELD (1897-1959)

negro parade

new york 7 april 1942	nbc symphony	cd: enno riekena (germany)

the mountain song

new york 28-29 april 1968	american symphony	cd: theo van der burg (netherlands)

FRANZ VON SUPPE (1819-1895)

die schöne galathea, overture

los angeles 11 august 1946	hollywood bowl symphony	unpublished recording

CARLOS SURINACH (born 1915)

melorhythmic dramas

new york 7 october 1968	american symphony	unpublished recording

BOLESLAW SZABELSKI (1896-1979)

toccata for orchestra

chicago 2 january 1958	chicago symphony	unpublished recording

DEEMS TAYLOR (1885-1966)

ballet music from raymuntcho

new york 26 december 1943	nbc symphony	unpublished recording

PIOTR TCHAIKOVSKY (1840-1893)

symphony no 4

camden nj march 1921	philadelphia orchestra	victor unpublished *third movement only*
philadelphia 28-29 september 1928	philadelphia orchestra	78: victor M 48 78: hmv DB 1793-1797/DB 7281-7285 cd: pearl GEMMCD 9120 *recording completed on 8 december 1928*
new york 1941	all-american symphony	columbia (usa) unpublished
new york 21 november 1941	nbc symphony	unpublished rehearsal recording
new york 25 november 1941	nbc symphony	cd: enno riekena (germany)
new york 27 november 1941	nbc symphony	78: victor M 880 lp: american stokowski society LSSA 1 lp: japanese stokowski society JLSS 4-5 cd: allegro CDO 1012 cd: grammofono AB 78836 cd: cala CACD 0505
los angeles 1 september 1946	hollywood bowl symphony	unpublished recording
new york january 1957	his symphony orchestra	lp: capitol P 8385/P 8673/SP 8385/ lp: angel seraphim 6094 cd: emi CDM 565 6142 *this recording was of the third movement only*
new york 3-6 april 1964	american symphony	unpublished video recording *rehearsal was apparently also recorded*

tokyo 8 july 1965	japan philharmonic	lp: japanese stokowski society JLSS 4-5
new york 23-27 april 1971	american symphony	unpublished recording *rehearsal was apparently also recorded*
new york 26 april 1971	american symphony	lp: vanguard VCS 10095 cd: vanguard OVC 8012/08.616271/ ATMCD 11902

symphony no 5

camden nj march 1923	philadelphia orchestra	victor unpublished *second movement only*
camden nj 30 april 1923	philadelphia orchestra	78: victor 74846-74848/6430-6431 *second movement only*
camden nj 12 november 1934	philadelphia orchestra	78: victor M 253 78: hmv DB 2548-2553/DB 7905-7910 lp: rca camden CAL 201 cd: biddulph WHL 015 cd: allegro CDO 1012 cd: grammofono AB 78713-78714 cd: iron needle IN 1367 cd: magic master MM 37089 cd: aura CD 258 cd: cantus classics 500.150 cd: history 20.3290 *CAL 201 named performers as warwick symphony orchestra*
philadelphia 1937	philadelphia orchestra	film soundtrack recording of fourth movement *one hundred men and a girl*
new york 29 november 1942	nbc symphony	unpublished recording
los angeles 27 august 1946	hollywood bowl symphony	unpublished recording

tchaikovsky/symphony no 5/concluded

new york 28 march 1947	his symphony orchestra	78: victor 11-9574 45: victor 49-0296 *this abridged version was described as "themes from the second movement" and was recorded as soundtrack to the film "carnegie hall"*
new york 13 november 1949	new york philharmonic	unpublished recording
hamburg 7 july 1952	ndr orchestra	lp: movimento musica 01.041 cd: frequenz 041.011 cd: archipel ARPCD 0087 cd: enno riekena (germany) cd: tahra TAH 485-486
detroit 20 november 1952	detroit symphony	unpublished recording
new york 10-12 february 1953	his symphony orchestra	lp: victor LM 1780 *apparently also issued on cd in japan*
stuttgart 20 may 1955	sdr orchestra	cd: refrain (japan) DR 930051
london 10 september 1966	new philharmonia	unpublished recording
london 13-16 september 1966	new philharmonia	lp: decca LK 4882/PFS 4129/SDD 493 lp: london (usa) SPC 21017 cd: decca 433 6872/475 1452
new york 3-4 december 1967	american symphony	cd: music and arts CD 944
geneva 19 august 1973	international youth festival	lp: cameo classics GOCLP 9007 cd: theo van der burg (netherlands) *recording also includes rehearsal extracts*

tchaikovsky/**symphony no 6 "pathétique"**

camden nj december 1917	philadelphia orchestra	victor unpublished *third movement only*
camden nj may 1919	philadelphia orchestra	victor unpublished *second movement only*
camden nj december 1920	philadelphia orchestra	victor unpublished *third movement only*
camden nj february 1921	philadelphia orchestra	victor unpublished *third movement only*
camden nj 18 march 1921	philadelphia orchestra	78: victor 74713/6242 *third movement only*
camden nj 8 december 1925	philadelphia orchestra	cd: biddulph BID 83072 *unpublished victor 78rpm recording described as andante theme from first movement*
new york 16 november 1940	all-american symphony	78: columbia (usa) M 432 78: columbia (canada) D 32
new york 30 january 1944	nbc symphony	unpublished recording
los angeles 25 july 1945	hollywood bowl symphony	78: victor M 1105 lp: rca camden CAL 152/CFL 100/CFL 104 lp: british stokowski society LS 9 cd: pearl GEMMCD 9261 cd: history 205.652303 cd: archipel ARPCD 0095 cd: cala CACD 0506 *rca camden issues named performers as star symphony orchestra*

tchaikovsky/symphony no 6/concluded

moscow 17 june 1958	ussr large radio symphony	cd: scora CD 009
new york 21-24 january 1966	american symphony	unpublished recording *rehearsal was apparently also recorded*
london 21 april 1973	london symphony	cd: music and arts CD 994
london 25 april 1973	london symphony	unpublished recording
london 5-10 september 1973	london symphony	lp: rca ARL1-0426 lp: grandi interpreti GIM 10 cd: rca bmg 09026 626022/09026 684432

piano concerto no 1

los angeles 25 august 1946	hollywood bowl symphony magadow, piano	cd: enno riekena (germany) *only first movement of the concerto was performed at this concert*
saarbrücken july 1969	saarbrücken radio orchestra leimer, piano	unpublished video recording

piano concerto no 2

los angeles 4 august 1946	hollywood bowl symphony cherkassky, piano	cd: pearl GEM 0138 *only second and third movements of the concerto were performed at this concert*

violin concerto

new york 7 may 1972	american symphony perlman, violin	cd: venezia (japan) V 1004

valse-scherzo

los angeles 11 august 1946	hollywood bowl symphony stockton, marimba	unpublished recording

tchaikovsky/**1812 overture**

camden nj 29-30 april 1930	philadelphia orchesrrea	78: victor 7499-7500 78: hmv DB 1663-1664 cd: biddulph WHL 015
london 15 june 1969	royal philharmonic grenadiers band alldis and welsh national opera choirs	cd: music and arts CD 847/CD 944 cd: bbc legends BBCL 40692
london 16-17 june 1969	royal philharmonic grenadiers band alldis and welsh national opera choirs	lp: decca PFS 4189/SDD 454 lp: decca (germany) 642.743 lp: london (usa) SPC 21041/SPC 21108 STS 15558 cd: decca 430 4102/433 6252/436 5062/ 443 8962/467 8282/475 6090

andante cantabile from string quartet no 1

new york 19 february 1958	his symphony orchestra	lp: capitol P 8458/P 8650/SP 8458/ SP 8650 lp: emi SXLP 30174 cd: emi CDM 565 9122 *recording completed on 26 february and 4 may 1958*

capriccio italien

philadelphia 28-30 january 1929	philadelphia orchestra	78: victor 6949-6950 78: hmv D 1739-1740/DB 6005-6006 78: hmv (italy) AW 201-202 L 7002 cd: pearl GEMMCD 9120 cd: history 205.652303 *L 7002 was an experimental 33.1/3 rpm issue (symphonic transcription disc)*
new york 25-26 march 1972	american symphony	unpublished recording *rehearsal was apparently also recorded*
london 4 november 1973	london philharmonic	unpublished recording
wembley 6-8 december 1973	london philharmonic	lp: philips 6500 766/6527 079/6770 053 lp: philips (usa) PHCP 9552/PHCP 9745 cd: philips 438 3862/442 7452

tchaikovsky/**casse noisette, suite from the ballet**

camden nj october 1917	philadelphia orchestra	victor unpublished *russian dance and dance of the sugar plum fairy only*
camden nj february 1921	philadelphia orchestra	victor unpublished *waltz of the flowers and dance of the reeds only*
camden nj april 1921	philadelphia orchestra	victor unpublished *dance of the reeds only*
camden nj 13 february 1922	philadelphia orchestra	78: victor 66128/798 *dance of the reeds only*
philadelphia 3 november 1926	philadelphia orchestra	78: victor M 3 78: hmv D 1214-1216/D 7390-7392 78: hmv (france) W 848-850 L 7004 cd: pearl GEMMCD 9488 cd: biddulph WHL 047 cd: andante 2985 *recording completed on 10 and 18 november 1926; L 7004 was an experimental 33.1/3 rpm issue (symphonic transcription disc)*
camden nj 26 november 1938	philadelphia orchestra	78: victor M 265 78: hmv DB 2540-2542 45: rca camden CAE 187 lp: rca camden CAL 100/CFL 102 cd: grammofono AB 78586 cd: archipel ARPCD 0095 cd: history 20.3290 cd: cala CACD 0521 *rca camden issues named performers as warwick symphony orchestra*

philadelphia april 1939	philadelphia orchestra	*fantasia soundtrack recording* lp: top rank 30-003 lp: disneyland WDL 4101/ST 3926/STER 101 lp: buena vista BVS 101 cd: buena vista CD 020/60007 cd: pony canyon PCCD 00009 cd: avex AVCW 12048-12049/12163-12164 cd: pickwick DSTCD 452 cd: documents 221708 vhs video: buena vista D 211322 vhs video: disneyland 101 dvd video: disney classics ZIDD 888113/888055
los angeles 21 july 1946	hollywood bowl symphony	cd: enno riekena (germany)
new york 2 march 1949	his symphony orchestra	78: victor M 1468 45: victor WDM 1468 lp: victor LM 46/LM 9023 lp: hmv ALP 1193 lp: hmv (france) FBLP 1002 lp: hmv (italy) QBLP 1002 lp: rca ANL1-2604 cd: otaken (japan) TK 5004 *excerpts from the suite* 78: victor 10-1487 78: hmv DB 21547 45: victor WDM 1394/49-0553/49-3346 45: hmv 7ER 5016/7RF 195 45: hmv (france) 7RF 195 45: hmv (italy) 7RQ 102 lp: victor LM 1083/VIC 1020 lp: hmv ALP 1133 *recording completed on 29 june 1950*
london 4 november 1973	london philharmonic	unpublished recording
wembley 6-8 december 1973	london philharmonic	lp: philips 6500 766/6527 027/6527 079/6770 053 lp: philips (usa) PHCP 9745/PHCP 9552 cd: philips 438 3862/442 7352

tchaikovsky/**chant sans paroles**

camden nj november- december 1922	philadelphia orchester	victor unpublished
camden nj 28 april 1924	philadelphia orchestra	78: victor 1111
philadelphia 8-9 december 1928	philadelphia orchestra	78: victor M 71/M 192 78: hmv D 1994/DB 2207 78: hmv (france) W 1186 78: hmv (italy) AW 263 lp: american stokowski society LSSA 1 cd: pearl GEMMCD 9120 cd: biddulph WHL 015
new york 23 march 1971	american symphony	unpublished recording
london 15 june 1972	london symphony	lp: decca PFS 4351 lp: london (usa) SPC 21130 cd: pickwick IMPX 9033 cd: decca 433 8762/475 1452

evgeny onegin, tatiana's letter scene

new york 6 february 1951	his symphony orchestra albanese	45: victor WDM 1610 lp: victor LM 142 lp: hmv BLP 1075 cd: rca/bmg GD 60384 cd: cala CACD 0540

evgeny onegin, waltz

london 4 november 1973	london philharmonic	unpublished recording
wembley 6-8 december 1973	london philharmonic	lp: philips 6500 766/6527 079/6570 027/ 6770 053 cd: philips 442 7352

tchaikovsky/**evgeny onegin, polonaise**

new york 1 october 1953	his symphony orchestra	lp: victor LM 2042 lp: japanese srokowski society JLSS 17 cd: theo van der burg (netherlands)
wembley 6-8 december 1973	london philharmonic	lp: philips 6500 766/6527 079/6570 027/ 6770 053 cd: philips 442 7352

francesca da rimini

los angeles 23 july 1946	hollywood bowl symphony	unpublished recording
new york 3 november 1947	new york philharmonic	78: columbia (usa) M 806 lp: columbia (usa) ML 4071/ML 4381/ P 14137 lp: columbia 33CX 1030 lp: columbia (italy) 33QCX 10001 cd: theo van der burg (netherlands) cd: cala CACD 0533
new york 7 october 1958	new york philharmonic	lp: everest LPBR 6011/SDBR 3011 lp: world records T 98/ST 98 lp: top rank 35-014 lp: dell' arte DA 9006 cd: priceless D 25327 cd: dell' arte CDDA 9006 cd: virtuoso 3602 cd: everest EVC 9037 *orchestra described for this recording as stadium symphony orchestra*
london 17 september 1964	london symphony	cd: theo van der burg (netherlands)
new york 26 october 1969	american symphony	unpublished recording
london 7 january 1974	london symphony	unpublished recording
wembley 9-13 october 1974	london symphony	lp: philips 6500 921/6770 053 cd: philips 442 7352 *also issued as sacd by pentatone*

tchaikovsky/**hamlet, fantasy overture**

new york 7 october 1958	new york philharmonic	lp: everest LPBR 6011/SDBR 3011 lp: world records T 98/ST 98 lp: top rank 35-014 lp: dell' arte DA 9006 cd: priceless D 25327 cd: dell' arte CDDA 9006 cd: virtuoso 3602 cd: everest EVC 9037 *orchestra was described for this recording as stadium symphony orchestra*
london 30 june 1959	london symphony	cd: theo van der burg (netherlands)
boston 13 january 1968	boston symphony	cd: boston symphony orchestra CB 101-112
new york 9-10 march 1969	american symphony	unpublished recording

humoresque

new york 10 july 1941	all-american symphony	78: columbia (usa) 19005 lp: japanese stokowski society JLSS 4-5 cd: theo van der burg (netherlands)
new york 23 april 1942	nbc symphony	78: victor M 933 cd: cala CACD 0505
los angeles 25 august 1946	hollywood bowl symphony	78: victor 11-9187 lp: rca camden CAL 153 *CAL 153 named performers as star symphony orchestra*
new york 25 february 1953	his symphony orchestra	lp: victor LM 1774
west ham july 1976	national philharmonic	lp: cbs 34543/73589 cd: cala CACD 0529

tchaikovsky/**hymn of praise** *also known as cherubic hymn no 1*

camden nj june 1922	choir	unpublished victor experimental recording

marche slave

philadelphia 15 may 1925	philadelphia orchestra	78: victor 6513 78: hmv D 1046 78: hmv (italy) AW 3398 cd: biddulph BID 83072 *apparently also issued in japan on an lp edition*
new york 23 april 1942	nbc symphony	cd: grammofono AB 78713-78714 cd: iron needle IN 1367 cd: magic master MM 37031 cd: aura 258 cd: allegro CDO 1012 cd: history 205.652303 cd: cantus classics 500.090 cd: cala CACD 0502 *unpublished victor 78rpm recording*
los angeles 1 august 1945	hollywood bowl symphony	78: victor 11-9388 lp: rca camden CAL 153 cd: pearl GEMMCD 9261 *CAL 153 named performers as star symphony orchestra*
los angeles 26 august 1946	hollywood bowl symphony	lp: japanese stokowski society JLSS 18 cd: theo van der burg (netherlands)
london 15 june 1967	london symphony	unpublished recording
london 16 june 1967	london symphony	lp: decca LK 4927/PFS 4139/D94 D2/ SDD 454/SPA 159 lp: london (usa) SPC 21026 lp: musical heritage society MHS 827052 cd: pickwick IMPX 9033 cd: decca 421 6342/430 4102/433 6252/ 443 8962/475 6090
london 14 june 1972	london symphony	unpublished video recording *bbc television*
london 15 june 1972	london symphony	lp: decca OPFS 3-4 lp: london (usa) SPC 21090-2191 cd: cala CACD 0536

tchaikovsky/**pater noster** *also known as church song no 3*

camden nj june 1922	choir	unpublished victor experimental recording *versions were made with and without stokowski playing an organ accompaniment*
london 19-20 july 1961	new symphony luboff choir	lp: victor LM 2593/LSC 2593 cd: rca/bmg 09026 625992/09026 684432

romeo and juliet, fantasy overture

philadelphia 26-27 september 1928	philadelphia orchestra	78: victor M 46 78: hmv D 1947-1949 cd: pearl GEMMCD 9120
new york 16 january 1944	nbc symphony	unpublished recording
new york 11 december 1944	new york city symphony	cd: grammofono AB 78713-78714 cd: magic master MM 37031 cd: iron needle IN 1367 cd: allegro CDO 1012 cd: aura 258 cd: history 20.3290 cd: cantus classics 500.090 cd: cala CACD 0502 *unpublished victor 78rpm recording*
new york 28 november 1949	new york philharmonic	78: columbia (usa) M 898 lp: columbia (usa) ML 4273/ML 4381/ ML 4071 lp: columbia 33CX 1030 lp: columbia (italy) 33QCX 10001 cd: cala CACD 0537
scheveningen 27 june 1951	residentie orchestra	cd: music and arts CD 831 cd: theo van der burg (netherlands) cd: archipel ARPCD 0087
philadelphia 6 february 1962	philadelphia orchestra	lp: grandi concerti GCL 57 cd: philadelphia orchestra POA 100

copenhagen 4 august 1967	danish radio orchestra	unpublished recording
lugano 7 august 1968	swiss-italian radio orchestra	cd: eremitage ERM 139/AUR 108/AUR 149 *also unpublished video recording*
geneva 11 september 1968	suisse romande orchestra	cd: theo van der burg (netherlands)
geneva 11-12 september 1968	suisse romande orchestra	lp: decca PFS 4181/SDD 454 lp: london (usa) SPC 21032/SPC 21108 lp: musical heritage society MHS 827052 cd: decca 433 6872/436 5312/448 9502
st moritz 30 august 1969	international youth festival orchestra	unpublished video recording
new york 7 march 1971	syracuse symphony	unpublished recording

serenade for strings

new york 16 january 1965	american symphony	unpublished rehearsal recording
london 7 january 1974	london symphony	unpublished recording
wembley 12-13 october 1974	london symphony	lp: philips 6500 921/6570 027/6770 053 lp: philips (usa) PHCP 9475/PHCP 9552 cd: philips 438 6092/442 7352 *also issued as sacd by pentatone*

tchaikovsky/**waltz from serenade for strings**

los angeles 2 september 1945	hollywood bowl symphony	lp: kensington (usa) M 1030
new york 28 november 1949	new york philharmonic	78: columbia (usa) M 898 cd: cala CACD 0534

the sleeping beauty, selections from the ballet

los angeles 18 august 1946	hollywood bowl symphony	victor unpublished
new york 11-14 december 1947	his symphony orchestra	78: victor M 1205/V 16 78: hmv DB 9499-9504 45: victor WDM 1205 lp: victor LM 1010 lp: hmv ALP 1002 lp: hmv (france) FALP 133 lp: hmv (italy) QALP 133 lp: british srokowski society LS 7 cd: iron needle IN 1334 cd: sirio SO 530010 cd: cala CACD 0522 *IN 1334 incorrectly dated 1934*
new york 8-9 april 1953	his symphony orchestra	lp: victor LM 1774 cd: rediscovery RD 009 *recording completed on 14 april 1953; this selection comprised second act of the ballet (aurora's wedding)*
london 10 september 1965	new philharmonia	cd: bbc legends BBCL 41152
london 11 september 1965	new philharmonia	lp: decca LK 4807/PFS 4083/SDD 454/ SPA 159/VIV 10 lp: decca (germany) 642.718 lp: london (usa) PM 55006/SPC 21008 cd: decca 430 1402/448 9502
west ham may 1976	national philharmonic	lp: cbs 34560/44560/76665 cd: cala CACD 0529 *this selection comprised the second act of the ballet (aurora's wedding)*

tchaikovsky/**solitude**

philadelphia 16 november 1936	philadelphia orchestra	78: victor 14947/M 710 78: hmv DB 3255 cd: biddulph WHL 015 cd: andante 2985
new york 11 july 1941	all-american symphony	78: columbia (usa) 11982
new york 20 february 1944	nbc symphony	unpublished recording
new york 11 may 1944	nbc symphony	cd: magic master MM 37031 cd: history 20.3290 cd: cantus classics 500.090 cd: cala CACD 0502 *unpublished victor 78rpm recording*
los angeles 25 july 1945	hollywood bowl symphony	78: victor 11-9187 lp: rca camden CAL 153 cd: pearl GEMMCD 9261 *CAL 153 named performers as star symphony orchestra*
new york 25 february 1953	his symphony orchestra	lp: victor LM 1774
new york 4 may 1969	american symphony	unpublished recording
west ham november 1975	national philharmonic	lp: pye nixa PCNHX 4 lp: vogue VC 25013 cd: pye nixa CDPCN 4 cd: emi CDM 764 1402

tchaikovsky/**swan lake, music from acts 2 and 3**

new york 20-21 october 1954	nbc symphony	lp: victor LM 1894 lp: hmv ALP 1443 lp: quintessence PMC 7007 cd: venezia (japan) V 1003 cd: theo van der burg (netherlands) cd: cala CACD 0543 *recording completed on 10 november 1954, 13 january 1955 and 10 february 1955; venezia issue incorrectly names orchestra as his symphony orchestra*

swan lake, suite from the ballet

new york 11 may 1950	his symphony orchestra	78: victor M 1394 45: victor WDM 1394 lp: victor LM 1083/VIC 1020 lp: hmv ALP 1133 cd: theo van der burg (netherlands) *this version comprises only dance of the cygnets and queen of the swans*
houston 5 november 1956	houston symphony	unpublished recording
chicago 9 january 1958	chicago symphony	unpublished recording
london 11 september 1965	new philharmonia	lp: decca LK 4807/PFS 4083/SPA 159/VIV 10 lp: london (usa) PM 55006/SPC 21008 cd: decca 430 1402/448 9502 *recording completed on 15 september 1965*
new york 6-7 may 1967	american symphony	unpublished recording *rehearsal was apparently also recorded*

the tempest, symphonic fantasy

new york 29 november 1942	nbc symphony	unpublished recording
new york 7 march 1943	nbc symphony	cd: enno riekena (germany)

GEORG PHILIPP TELEMANN (1681-1767)

overture in d

new york 21 january 1966	american symphony	unpublished rehearsal recording
new york 24 november 1969	american symphony	unpublished recording

AMBROISE THOMAS (1811-1896)

raymonde, overture

los angeles 4 august 1946	hollywood bowl symphony	unpublished recording

gavotte from mignon

camden nj 1 may 1923	philadelphia orchestra	78: victor 66172/944 78: hmv DA 562
philadelphia 4 may 1929	philadelphia orchestra	78: victor M 116 78: hmv DB 1643 cd: biddulph WHL 011 cd: magic talent MT 48015 cd: magic master MM 37022 cd: cantus classics 500.090 *cd re-issues incorrectly dated 1937*

VIRGIL THOMSON (1896-1989)

cantabile for strings

new york 25 october 1953	cbs studio orchestra	cd: enno riekena (germany)

fugues and cantilenas

baltimore 10 january 1963	baltimore symphony	unpublished recording

the mother of us all, symphonic suite

new york 2 april 1950	new york philharmonic	lp: new york philharmonic NYP 821-822

the plow that broke the plains, suite

new york 16 january 1944	nbc symphony	unpublished recording
los angeles 27 august 1946	hollywood bowl symphony	unpublished recording
los angeles 30 august 1946	hollywood bowl symphony	78: victor M 1116 cd: rca/bmg 09026 681632
new york 21 december 1960	symphony of the air	lp: vanguard VRS 1071/VSD 2095/ VSD 385/VSD 707-708 lp: analogue productions APC 001 cd: vanguard OVC 8013/SVC 1 *also issued as sacd by vanguard*

the river, suite

new york 21 december 1960	symphony of the sir	lp: vanguard VRS 1071/VSD 2095/ VSD 385/VSD 707-708 lp: analogue productions APC 101 cd: vanguard OVC 8013/SVC 1 *also issued as sacd by vanguard*

sea piece for birds

new york 3-4 april 1970	american symphony	cd: theo van der burg (netherlands)

thomson/**the seine at night**

new york 21 march 1948	new york philharmonic	unpublished recording
new york 1 october 1965	american symphony	unpublished rehearsal recording

shipwreck and love scene from byron's don juan

new york 13 april 1968	new york philharmonic kness, piano	unpublished recording

tango

new york 12 october 1971	american symphony	cd: theo van der burg (netherlands)

MICHAEL TIPPETT (1905-1998)

concerto for double string orchestra

edinburgh 22 august 1961	london symphony	cd: bbc legends BBCL 40592

ERNST TOCH (1887-1964)

pinoccio, overture

los angeles 28 july 1946	hollywood bowl symphony	cd: theo van der burg (netherlands)

HAROLD TRIGGS

the bright land

new york 15 november 1942	nbc symphony	unpublished recording

JOAQUIN TURINA (1882-1949)

danzas fantasticas

los angeles 30 july 1946	hollywood bowl symphony	unpublished recording

gypsy dance from the sacred mountain

philadelphia 5 april 1937	philadelphia orchestra	cd: japanese stokowski society LSCD 20 cd: cala CACD 0501 cd: cantus classics 500.090 *unpublished victor 78rpm recording*

la oracion del torero

los angeles 18 august 1946	hollywood bowl symphony	unpublished recording
new york 19 february 1958	his symphony orchestra	lp: capitol P 8458/P 8694/SP 8694 lp: angel 34481 lp: angel seraphim 6094 lp: emi SXLP 30174 cd: emi 575 4812

SERGEI VASSILENKO (1872-1956)

hyrcus nocturnus

philadelphia 12 march 1932	philadelphia orchestra	bell telephone unpublished

RALPH VAUGHAN WILLIAMS (1872-1958)

symphony no 4

new york 14 march 1943	nbc symphony	cd: cala CACD 0528

symphony no 6 *original version*

new york 21 february 1949	new york philharmonic	78: columbia (usa) M 838 lp: columbia (usa) ML 4214 lp: cbs 61432 cd: sony SMK 58933/SBK 62754 cd: retrospective RET 011 cd: cala CACD 0537

vaughan williams/**symphony no 8**

new york 22 february 1957	his symphony orchestra	lp: capitol P 8385 cd: emi CDM 565 6142 *this recording was of the scherzo movement only; recording completed on 29 february 1957*
london 15 september 1964	bbc symphony	cd: music and arts CD 770 cd: nippon crown (japan) CRCB 6041 cd: bbc radio classsics 15656 91312 cd: bbc legends BBCL 41652

symphony no 9

new york 25 september 1958	his symphony orchestra	cd: cala CACD 0539

variants of dives and lazarus

new york february 1954	cbs studio orchestra	cd: enno riekena (germany)

fantasia on christmas carols

new york 19 december 1943	nbc symphony	unpublished recording

fantasia on greensleeves

new york 21 february 1949	new york philharmonic	78: columbia (usa) M 838 lp: columbia (usa) BM 13 lp: japanese stokowski society JLSS 19 cd: theo van der burg (netherlands) cd: cala CACD 0533 *rehearsal extracts were apparently also recorded*
london 17 september 1964	london symphony	cd: theo van der burg (netherlands)

vaughan williams/**fantasia on a theme by thomas tallis**

new york 25-28 march 1948	new york philharmonic	lp: japanese stokowski society JLSS 19 cd: theo van der burg (netherlands)
new york 3 september 1952	his symphony orchestra	45: victor WDM 1739 lp: victor LM 1739 lp: hmv ALP 1205 lp: british stokowski society LS 17 cd: cala CACD 0533
new york 17 november 1960	symphony of the air	cd: library of congress CLS 2 cd: bridge 9074
new york 2 march 1962	new york philharmonic	unpublished recording
london 14 may 1974	new philharmonia	cd: bbc radio classics BBCRD 9107 cd: crown nippon (japan) CRCB 6017
london 16-19 august 1975	royal philharmonic	lp: desmar DSM 1011 lp: decca (germany) 642.631 cd: emi 566 7602

TOMAS LUIS DE VICTORIA (1548-1611)

jesu dulcis memoria

new york 5 january 1947	new york philharmonic	unpublished recording
philadelphia 13 february 1969	philadelphia orchestra	unpublished recording

GIUSEPPE VERDI (1813-1901)

te deum/4 pezzi sacri

new york 17 december 1967	american symphony orchestra and chorus	unpublished recording

ciel mio padre!/aida

philadelphia 20 january 1962	philadelphia orchestra nilsson london	lp: melodram MEL 228 cd: bella voce BLV 107.235

ella giammai m' amo/don carlo

los angeles 19 august 1945	hollywood bowl symphony moscona	unpublished recording

la forza del destino, overture

philadelphia 19 january 1963	philadelphia orchestra	lp: japanese stokowski society JLSS 11-12 cd: bella voce BLV 107.235

il lacerato spirto/simon boccanegra

los angeles 25 august 1946	hollywood bowl symphony ford	cd: enno riekena (germany)

brindisi/la traviata

philadelphia 1936	philadelphia orchestra durbin	film soundtrack recording *one hundred men and a girl*

HENRI VIEUXTEMPS (1820-1880)

violin concerto no 4

new york 22-23 march 1969	american symphony kim, violin	unpublished recording

HEITOR VILLA-LOBOS (1887-1959)

guitar concerto

new york 16-18 november 1968	american symphony diaz, guitar	unpublished recording *rehearsal was apparently also recorded*

cancao do carreiro/serestas

new york 3 april 1967	american symphony godoy	unpublished recording

uirapuru, tone poem

new york 8 october 1958	new york philharmonic	lp: everest LPBR 6016/SDBR 3016 cd: priceless D 24924 cd: everest EVC 9023 *orchestra described for this recording as stadium symphony*
new york 3 april 1967	american symphony	unpublished recording

bachianas brasilieras no 1 "modinha"

new york 8 october 1958	new york philharmonic	lp: everest LPBR 6016/SDBR 3016 lp: world records T 173/ST 173 cd: priceless D 24924 cd: everest EVC 9023 *orchestra described for this recording as stadium symphony*
new york 5 october 1963	american symphony	unpublished rehearsal recording

bachianas brasilieras no 2

los angeles 18 august 1946	hollywood bowl symphony	unpublished recording

bachianas brasilieras no 5

new york 6-8 february 1951	his symphony orchestra albanese	lp: victor LM 142 lp: hmv BLP 1075 lp: hmv (italy) QBLP 1025
new york 13 april 1964	american symphony moffo	lp: victor LSC 2795/LSB 4114 lp: victor (france) 635.040 cd: rca/bmg GD 87831/09026 626002/ 09026 684432/74321 709312
new york 3 april 1967	american symphony godoy	unpublished recording

ANTONIO VIVALDI (1675-1741)

le 4 stagioni

london 11 june 1966	new philharmonia bean, violin	lp: decca LK 4873/PFS 4124/VIV 3 lp: london (usa) SPC 21015/STS 15539 cd: decca 417 0742/433 6802 cd: cala CACD 0538
london june 1966	new philharmonia bean, violin	unpublished recording

concerto in b minor for 4 violins

los angeles 5 august 1945	hollywood bowl symphony ayres, weinstein, warner, schaeffer, violins	unpublished recording

concerto in d minor op 3 no 11

camden nj 12 november 1934	philadelphia orchestra	78: victor 14113-14114 78: hmv DB 6047-6048 lp: american stokowski society LSSA 5 cd: theo van der burg (netherlands) cd: music and arts CD 1173
los angeles 20 august 1946	hollywood bowl symphony	unpublished recording
new york 28-29 february 1952	his symphony orchestra	45: victor WDM 1721 lp: victor LM 1721
philadelphia 4 february 1964	philadelphia orchestra	unpublished recording
boston 6 march 1964	boston symphony	unpublished recording
new york 19-21 april 1967	his symphony orchestra kipnis, harpsichord	lp: bach guild 70696 lp: vanguard SRV 363/VSD 707-708 cd: vanguard OVC 8009/VBD 363

JOHN WADE (1711-1786)

o come all ye faithful

camden nj june 1922	choir	unpublished victor experimental recording *versions made with and without stokowski playing organ part*
new york 1944	westminster choir	unpublished video recording

RICHARD WAGNER (1813-1883)

siegfried idyll

new york 6 december 1942	nbc symphony	unpublished recording
new york 17 november 1960	symphony of the air	cd: library of congress CLC 2 cd: music and arts CD 657 cd: bridge 9074

wesendonk-lieder

philadelphia 22 december 1940	philadelphia orchestra traubel	78: victor M 872 lp: neiman marcus (usa) cd: pearl GEMMCD 9486 cd: preiser 89120 cd: andante 1130 *only three of the songs were recorded (im treibhaus; schmerzen; träume)*
new york 22 may 1950	his symphony orchestra farrell	78: victor M 1233 45: victor WDM 1233 lp: victor LM 1066/AVM1-1413 cd: theo van der burg (netherlands) cd: testament awaiting publication
new york 6-8 december 1969	american symphony lindholm	unpublished recording *rehearsal was apparently also recorded*
new york 14 november 1971	american symphony jung	unpublished recording

der fliegende holländer, overture

new york 21 february 1949	new york philharmonic	lp: columbia (usa) BM 39 lp: japanese stokowski society JLSS 19 cd: theo van der burg (netherlands) cd: cala CACD 0533
new york 24 april 1965	american symphony	unpublished rehearsal recording
philadelphia 21 june 1965	philadelphia orchestra	unpublished recording
new york 14 november 1971	american symphony	unpublished recording

wagner/**dawn and rhine journey/götterdämmerung**

philadelphia 29-30 april 1932	philadelphia orchestra	bell telephone unpublished
camden nj 25-29 march 1933	philadelphia orchestra	78: victor M 188 78: hmv DB 2126-2130/DB 7621-7625 cd: pearl GEMMCDS 9076 cd: grammofono AB 78766-78767 cd: andante 1130 *recording completed on 28 october 1933*
los angeles 14 july 1946	hollywood bowl symphony	unpublished recording
new york 4 april 1949	new york philharmonic	lp: columbia (usa) ML 4273 cd: cala CACD 0534
philadelphia 13 december 1963	philadelphia orchestra	lp: japanese stokowski society JLSS 18 cd: theo van der burg (netherlands)
london 26 august 1966	london symphony	lp: decca LK 4851/PFS 4116/SPA 537 lp: london (usa) SPC 21016/STS 15565 cd: decca 421 0202/433 6392/ 443 9012/475 6090
london 15 june 1967	london symphony	cd: bbc legends BBCL 40882
new york 8 december 1969	american symphony	unpublished recording
london 11-15 november 1974	london symphony	lp: rca ARL1-1317 cd: rca/bmg 09026 625982/09026 684432/ 82875 553062

wagner/**siegfried's death and funeral march/götterdämmerung**

camden nj november- december 1922	philadelphia orchestra	victor unpublished
philadelphia 29-30 april 1932	philadelphia orchestra	lp: bell telephone laboratories BTL 8001 cd: theo van der burg (netherlands)
camden nj 25-29 march 1933	philadelphia orchestra	78: victor M 188 78: hmv DB 2126-2130/DB 7621-7625 cd: pearl GEMMCDS 9076 cd: grammofono AB 78766-78767 cd: andante 1130 *recordeing completed on 28 october 1933*
new york 4 april 1949	new york philharmonic	lp: columbia (usa) ML 4273 cd: cala CACD 0534
philadelphia 13 december 1963	philadelphia orchestra	lp: japanese stokowski society JLSS 18 cd: theo van der burg (netherlands)
new york 21 december 1963	american symphony	unpublished recording
new york 3 april 1964	american symphony	unpublished recording
london 26 august 1966	london symphony	lp: decca LK 4851/PFS 4116 lp: london (usa) SPC 21016/STS 15565 cd: decca 421 0202/433 6392/ 443 9012/475 6090
london 15 june 1967	london symphony	cd: bbc legends BBCL 40882
new york 8 december 1969	american symphony	unpublished recording
london 11-15 november 1974	london symphony	lp: rca ARL1-1317 cd: rca/bmg 09026 625982/09026 684432/ 82875 553062

wagner/**starke scheite schichtet mir dort/götterdämmerung**

philadelphia 16-18 january 1932	philadelphia orchestra alsen	bell telephone unpublished *apparently two recordings were made*
philadelphia 29-30 april 1932	philadelphia orchestra	lp: bell telephone laboratories BTL 8001 *orchestral version without soloist*
camden nj 28 october 1933	philadelphia orchestra davies	78: victor M 188 78: hmv DB 2126-2130/DB 7621-7625 LM 188 lp: recherche 1002 cd: pearl GEMMCDS 9076 cd: grammofono AB 78766-78767 cd: andante 1130 *LM 188 was an experimental 33.1/3 rpm issue (symphonic transcription disc)*
new york 27 march 1949	new york philharmonic	unpublished recording *orchestral version without soloist*
philadelphia 20 january 1962	philadelphia orchestra nilsson	lp: melodram MEL 228 cd: philadelphia orchestra POA 100 cd: bella voce BLV 107.235
philadelphia 13 december 1963	philadelphia orchestra	lp: japanese stokowski society JLSS 18 cd: theo van der burg (netherlands) *orchestral version without soloist*
london 15 june 1967	london symphony lindholm	cd: bbc legends BBCL 40882
new york 14 november 1971	american symphony	unpublished recording *orchestral version without soloist*
london 11-15 november 1974	london symphony	lp: rca ARL1-1317/AGL1-3709 cd: rca/bmg 09026 625982/09026 684432 *orchestral version without soloist*

wagner/**götterdämmerung, orchestral postlude**

camden nj november- december 1922	philadelphia orchestra	victor unpublished
philadelphia 6 january 1927	philadelphia orchestra	78: victor 6625 78: hmv D 1227 78: hmv (france) W 1014 78: electrola EJ 159 lp: victor VCM 7101/VIC 6060 cd: pearl GEMMCDS 9076/GEMS 0024 cd: magic talent MT 48015 cd: magic masters MM 37022 cd: cantus classics 500.090 cd: history 20.3290 cd: theo van der burg (netherlands) cd: rca/bmg 09026 638612 cd: andante 1130

lohengrin, prelude

camden nj april 1922	philadelphia orchestra	victor unpublished
camden nj 28 april 1924	philadelphia orchestra	78: victor 6490 78: hmv DB 839
philadelphia 13 october 1927	philadelphia orchestra	78: victor 6791 78: hmv D 1463 78: hmv (france) W 986 78: electrola EJ 361 lp: rca camden CAL 120 lp: american stokowski society LSSA 2 cd: pearl GEMMCD 9486 cd: grammofono AB 78758-78759 cd: membran 222174 cd: history 20..3290 cd: andante 1130 *CAL 120 named performers as warwick symphony orchestra*
new york 23 january 1943	nbc symphony	unpublished recording

los angeles 16 july 1946	hollywood bowl symphony	unpublished recording
houston 18 march 1957	houston symphony	unpublished recording
moscow 17 june 1958	ussr large radio symphony	cd: scora CD 009
philadelphia 20 january 1962	philadelphia orchestra	lp: melodram MEL 228 cd: bella voce BLV 107.235 *melodram issue incorrectly labelled as act 2 prelude*
new york 6-8 december 1969	american symphony	unpublished recording *rehearsal was apparently also recorded*

wagner/lohengrin, act 3 prelude

camden nj may 1919	philadelphia orchestra	victor unpublished
camden nj march-april 1921	philadelphia orchestra	victor unpublished
philadelphia 8 december 1935	philadelphia orchestra	lp: japanese stokowski society JLSS 03
philadelphia 1936	philadelphia orchestra	film soundtrack recording *one hundred men and a girl*
philadelphia 27 march 1940	philadelphia orchestra	78: victor M 731 78: hmv DB 5853/DB 6041 cd: pearl GEMMCD 9486 cd: grammofono AB 78758-78759 cd: history 20.3290 cd: andante 1130
los angeles 31 october 1943	hollywood bowl canteen symphony	cd: theo van der burg (netherlands)
philadelphia 17 december 1962	philadelphia orchestra	cd: philadelphia orchestra POA 91 cd: theo van der burg (netherlands)
new york 21 december 1963	american symphony	unpublished rehearsal recording
new york 3 april 1964	american symphony	unpublished rehearsal recording
philadelphia 14 october 1966	philadelphia orchestra	unpublished recording
london 11 january 1973	new philharmonia	unpublished recording

wagner/die meistersinger von nürnberg, overture

philadelphia 15 january 1936	philadelphia orchestra	78: victor M 508/M 731 78: hmv DB 5852-5853/DB 6040-6041 lp: american stokowski society LSSA 2 cd: pearl GEMMCD 9486 cd: grammofono AB 78758-78759 cd: membran 222174 cd: history 20.3290 cd: andante 1130
croydon 23 september 1967	london symphony	cd: bbc legends BBCL 40882
new york 23-24 april 1971	american symphony	unpublished rehearsal recording
london 14 june 1972	london symphony	lp: decca OPFS 3-4 lp: london (usa) SPC 21090-21091 cd: decca 421 0202/433 6392/ 443 9012/475 6090

die meistersinger von nürnberg, act 3 prelude

camden nj 17 march 1931	philadelphia orchestra	78: victor 1584 78: hmv DA 1291 cd: pearl GEMMCD 9238 cd: grammofono AB 78758-78759 cd: history 20.3290 cd: andante 1130

other versions of act 3 prelude are included in the meistersinger suite (see opposite page)

wagner/**die meistersinger von nürnberg, act 3 suite**

comprises prelude, dance of the apprentices and entry of the masters

philadelphia 18 december 1964	philadelphia orchestra	cd: theo van der burg (netherlands)
croydon 23 september 1967	london symphony	cd: music and arts CD 943 cd: bbc legends BBCL 40882
new york 27 april 1971	american symphony	unpublished recording
london 30 september 1973	royal philharmonic	unpublished recording
barking 15-19 october 1973	royal philharmonic	lp: rca ARS1-0498 cd: rca/bmg 09026 612682/09026 625982/ 09026 684432/82875 553062

parsifal, prelude

philadelphia 28 november 1936	philadelphia orchestra	78: victor M 421 78: hmv DB 3269-3270 lp: rca camden CAL 163 cd: pearl GEMMCD 9448 *CAL 163 named performers as warwick symphony orchestra*
new york 28 march 1943	nbc symphony	unpublished recording

parsifal, act 3 prelude

new york 28 march 1943	nbc symphony	unpublished recording

wagner/parsifal, act 1 transformation music

camden nj may 1923	philadelphia orchestra	victor unpublished

parsifal, good friday music

philadelphia 28 november 1936	philadelphia orchestra	78: victor M 421 78: hmv DB 3271-3272 lp: rca camden CAL 163 cd: pearl GEMMCD 9448 cd: grammofono AB 78758-78759 cd: cantus classics 500.090 cd: history 20.3290 cd: andante 1130 *CAL 163 named performers as warwick symphony orchestra*
new york 31 march 1942	nbc symphony	unpublished recording
new york 17 september 1952	his symphony orchestra	lp: victor LM 1730 lp: british stokowski society LS 5 cd: cala CACD 0535
houston 26-28 march 1959	houston symphony	lp: everest LPBR 6031/SDBR 3031 lp: world records TP 79 lp: hallmark SHM 541 lp: top rank 40-007 lp: vox STGBY 515040 cd: everest EVC 9024

wagner/**parsial, symphonic synthesis of music from act 3**

philadelphia october 1933	philadelphia orchestra	unpublished recording
camden nj 7 april 1934	philadelphia orchestra	78: victor 8617-8618 78: hmv DB 2272-2273 cd: pearl GEMMCD 9448 cd: membran 222174 cd: history 20.3290 cd: andante 1130
new york 31 march 1942	nbc symphony	unpublished recording
new york 24 september 1952	his symphony orchestra	lp: victor LM 1730 lp: british stokowski society LS 5 cd: cala CACD 0535
houston 26-28 march 1959	houston symphony	lp: everest LPBR 6031/SDBR 3031 lp: world records TP 79 lp: hallmark SHM 541 lp: top rank 40-007 lp: vox STGBY 515040 cd: everest EVC 9024
new york 2 march 1962	new york philharmonic	unpublished recording
new york 13-18 april 1963	american symphony	unpublished recording *rehearsal was apparently also recorded*
new york 13 april 1968	new york philharmonic	unpublished recording

wagner/**parsifal, extracts from complete concert performances of the music drama**

philadelphia 31 march- 1 april 1933	philadelphia orchestra and choirs bampton steel eddy tcherkassky treash	lp: ed smith/unique opera recordings UORC 280 cd: theo van der burg (netherlands)

enno riekena also mentions recorded stokowski performances of further extracts from parsifal with new york city symphony orchestra (1944) and an unspecified orchestra (1945)

das rheingold, entry of the gods into valhalla

philadelphia 16 january 1932	philadelphia orchestra	bell telephone unpublished
philadelphia 1940	philadelphia orchestra	78: victor M 1063
los angeles 31 october 1943	hollywood bowl canteen symphony	cd: theo van der burg (netherlands)
new york 20-21 april 1961	symphony of the air arroyo ordassy parker	lp: victor LM 1336/LSC 2555/VCS 7077/ VICS 1301 lp: rca RB 16279/SB 2148/AGL1-1338/ GL 11336 lp: decca (germany) 648.297 lp: camden classics CCV 5005 cd: rca/bmg 09026 625972/09026 684432/ 82875 553062
london 26 august 1966	london symphony	lp: decca LK 4851/PFS 4116/SPA 537 lp: london (usa) SPC 21016/STS 15565 cd: decca 421 0202/425 7872/433 6392/ 443 9012/475 6090

another version of entry of the gods included in orchestral suite from das rheingold (see opposite page)

wagner/**das rheingold, orchestral suite**

comprises prelude, song of the rhinemaidens, alberich steals the gold, erda's warning and entry of the gods

camden nj may 1923	philadelphia orchestra	victor unpublished *alberich steals the gold and erda's waening only*
camden nj 4 march 1933	philadelphia orchestra	78: victor M 179 78: hmv DB 1976-1978/DB 7626-7628 L 11643-11644 cd: pearl GEMMCDS 9076 cd: grammofono AB 78758-78759 cd: andante 1130 *L 11643-11644 was an experimental 33.1/3 rpm issue (symphonic transcription disc)*

rienzi, overture

camden nj 8 may 1919	philadelphia orchestra	78: victor 74602-74603/6239 78: hmv 0520-0521/DB 382
philadelphia 18 november 1926	philadelphia orchestra	78: victor 6624-6625 78: hmv D 1226-1227 78: hmv (italy) AW 4028 and 4030 78: electrola EJ 158-159 lp: cameo classics GOCLP 9009 cd: pearl GEMMCD 9238 cd: grammofono AB 78758-78759 cd: history 20.3290 cd: andante 1130 *recording completed on 6 january 1927*
new york 4 august 1949	new york philharmonic	lp: columbia (usa) ML 2153 lp: columbia 33C 1026 lp: columbia (italy) 33QC 1027 cd: theo van der burg (netherlands) cd: cala CACD 0534
philadelphia 20 january 1962	philadelphia orchestra	lp: melodram MEL 228 cd: bella voce BLV 107.235
new york 6-7 may 1967	american symphony	unpublished recording *rehearsal was apparently also recorded*
london 18 june 1968	new philharmonia	cd: bbc legends BBCL 40882
london 19-20 june 1968	new philharmonia	decca unpublished
barking 15-19 october 1973	royal philharmonic	lp: rca ARS1-0498 cd: rca/bmg 09026 612682/09026 625972/ 09026 684432/82875 553062 *rehearsal extract and alternative ending* cd: rca/bmg 09026 684432

wagner/**siegfried, forest murmurs**

philadelphia 29-30 april 1932	philadelphia orchestra	lp: bell telephone laboratories BTL 8001 cd: theo van der burg (netherlands)
los angeles 15 august 1946	hollywood bowl symphony	78: victor 11-9418 78: hmv DB 21238 lp: rca camden CAL 153 cd: cala CACD 0520 *CAL 153 named performers as star symphony orchestra*
new york 18 april 1964	american symphony	unpublished rehearsal recording
london 26 august 1966	london symphony	lp: decca LK 4851/PFS 4116 lp: london (usa) SPC 21016/STS 15565 cd: decca 421 0202/425 7872/433 6392/ 443 9012/475 6090
new york 27-28 october 1968	american symphony	unpublished recording

another version of forest murmurs included in the set of extracts listed on opposite page

siegfried, orchestral entr' acte (siegfried's ascent to the rock)

philadelphia 29-30 april 1932	philadelphia orchestra	bell telephone unpublished

wagner/**siegfried, set of extracts**

comprises wanderer questions mime (orchestral), forging song, forest murmurs and final part of closing duet

camden nj 26 november 1934	philadelphia orchestra davies jagel	78: victor M 441 78: hmv DB 3678-3680 lp: recherche LP 1002 cd: pearl GEMMCDS 9076 cd: grammofono AB 78758-78759 cd: andante 1130 *recherche lp contains only final part of closing duet*

tannhäuser, overture (dresden version)

camden nj may 1919	philadelphia orchestra	victor unpublished
camden nj march 1921	philadelphia orchestra	victor unpublished
camden nj 7 november 1921	philadelphia orchestra	78: victor 74758-74759 and 74768/6244 and 6478 78: hmv DB 386-387 lp: british stokowski society LS 3 cd: andante 1130 *recording completed on 5 december 1921*
philadelphia 8 february 1963	philadelphia orchestra	unpublished recording

wagner/tannhäuser, overture and venusberg music (paris version)

philadelphia 23 september 1929	philadelphia orchestra	78: victor M 78 78: hmv D 1905-1907/D 7372-7374 78: electrola EJ 648-650 L 11669 11670 cd: pearl GEMMCD 9238 cd: andante 1130 *recording completed on 14 march 1930 and 29 april 1930; L 11669-11670 was an experimental 33.1/3 rpm issue (symphonic transcription disc)*
philadelphia 12 december 1938	philadelphia orchestra	78: victor M 530 78: hmv DB 3775 3777 cd: pearl GEMMCD 9448 cd: grammofono AB 78758-78759 cd: history 20.3290 cd: andante 1130
new york 1 february 1950	his symphony orchestra and chorus	78: victor M 1383 45: victor WDM 1383 lp: victor LM 1066 lp: british stokowski society LS 19 cd: theo van der burg (netherlands) *recording completed on 15 february 1950*
new york 28 december 1960	symphony of the air and chorus	lp: victor LM 1336/LSC 2555/VICS 1301/ AGL1-1338 lp: rca RB 16279/SB 2148/GL 11336 lp: camden classics CCV 5005 lp: quintessence PMC 7019 cd: rca/bmg 09026 615032/09026 625972/ 09026 684432 *quintessence incorrectly described orchestra as rca victor symphony*

wagner/**tannhäuser, act 3 prelude**

philadelphia 15 january 1936	philadelphia orchestra	78: victor M 530 78: hmv DB 3254-3255 cd: pearl GEMMCD 9448 cd: grammofono AB 78758 78759 cd: history 20.3290 cd: andante 1130
new york 1 february 1950	his symphony orchestra	78: victor M 1383 45: victor WDM 1383 lp: victor LM 1066 lp: british stokowski society LS 19 cd: theo van der burg (netherlands) *recording completed on 15 february 1950*

tannhäuser, entry of the guests (grand march)

camden nj april 1923	philadelphia orchestra	victor unpublished
camden nj december 1923	philadelphia orchestra	victor unpublished
camden nj 28 april 1924	philadelphia orchestra	78: victor 6478 lp: british stokowski society LS 3 cd: andante 1130
new york 16 april 1966	metropolitan opera orchestra and chorus	lp: mrf records MRF 7 lp: japanese stokowski society JLSS 03 *performed at farewell gala in the old metropolitan opera house and including stokowski's brief speech*

tannhäuser, pilgrims' chorus

london 19-20 july 1961	new symphony luboff choir	lp: victor LM 2593/LSC 2593/VCS 7077 lp: quintessence PMC 7019 cd: rca/bmg GD 89293/09026 625992/ 09026 684432

wagner/**tristan und isolde, prelude**

camden nj february 1922	philadelphia orchestra	victor unpublished
camden nj april 1922	philadelphia orchestra	victor unpublished
camden nj october 1922	philadelphia orchestra	victor unpublished
philadelphia 5 april 1937	philadelphia orchestra	78: victor 15202-15203/M 508 cd: pearl GEMMCD 9486 cd: andante 1130 *recording completed on 11 november 1937*

tristan und isolde, act 3 prelude

los angeles 16 july 1946	hollywood bowl symphony	unpublished recording
new york 20-21 april 1961	symphony of the air	lp: victor LM 1336/LSC 2555/VICS 1301/ AGL1-1338 lp: rca RB 16279/SB 2148/GL 11336 lp: camden classics CCV 5005 cd: rca/bmg 09026 615032/09026 625972/ 09026 684432

tristan und isolde, prelude and liebestod

philadelphia 19 december 1931	philadelphia orchestra	lp: bell telephone laboratories BTL 7901 cd: iron needle IN 1402 cd: theo van der burg (netherlands)
philadelphia 8 december 1935	philadelphia orchestra	unpublished recording
new york 22 november 1942	nbc symphony	unpublished recording
new york february 1945	new york city symphony	victor unpublished

wagner/tristan prelude and liebestod/concluded

los angeles 6 august 1946	hollywood bowl symphony	unpublished recording
stuttgart 20 may 1955	sdr orchestra	unpublished recording
moscow 17 june 1958	ussr large radio symphony	cd: scora CD 009
philadelphia 21 january 1962	philadelphia orchestra	lp: melodram MEL 228 cd: theo van der burg (netherlands)
baltimore 18 april 1966	baltimore symphony	unpublished recording
philadelphia 13 february 1969	philadelphia orchestra	unpublished recording
new york 8 december 1969	american orchestra lindholm	unpublished recording *rehearsal was apparently also recorded*
new york 14 november 1972	american symphony jung	unpublished recording
london 30 september 1973	royal philharmonic	unpublished recording
barking 15-19 october 1973	royal philharmonic	lp: rca ARS1-0498 cd: rca/bmg 09026 612682/09026 625982/ 09026 684432/82875 553062

wagner/tristan und isolde, symphonic synthesis

based on music from the second and third acts of the music drama

camden nj 16 april 1932	philadelphia orchestra	78: victor M 154 78: hmv DB 1911-1914/DB 7399-7402 L 11636-11637 cd: pearl GEMMCD 9328 cd: grammofono AB 78758-78759 cd: history 20.3290 cd: andante 1130 *recording completed on 23 april 1932; L 11636-11637 was an experimental 33.1/3 rpm issue (symphonic transcription disc)*
philadelphia 16 december 1935	philadelphia orchestra	78: victor M 508 78: hmv DB 3087-3089 lp: american stokowski society LSSA 2 cd: pearl GEMMCD 9486 cd: membran 222174 cd: andante 1130 *recording completed on 30 december 1935; final side of the recording (liebestod) was re-made on 20 april 1939*
new york november 1940	all-american symphony	78: columbia (usa) M 427
new york 28 february 1943	nbc symphony	unpublished recording
new york 2 january 1944	nbc symphony	unpublished recording
los angeles 29 july 1945	hollywood bowl symphony	unpublished recording
new york 17 october 1950	his symphony orchestra	45: victor WDM 1567 lp: victor LM 1174 lp: british stokowski society LS 19 cd: theo van der burg (netherlands) *recording completed on 9 november 1950*
philadelphia 23 february 1960	philadelphia orchestra	unpublished recording

wagner/tristan symphonic synthesis/concluded

philadelphia 25 february 1960	philadelphia orchestra	lp: columbia (usa) ML 5471/MS 6147/ MGP 17/Y-32368 lp: philips fontana CFL 1071/SCFL 107/ 699 062CL lp: cbs 61288 cd: philadelphia orchestra POA 100 cd: emi CZS 575 4802
new york 5 may 1968	american symphony	cd: memories HR 4495-4497

sink hernieder nacht der liebe/tristan und isolde

philadelphia 16-18 april 1932	philadelphia orchestra alsen bampton althouse	bell telephone unpublished *two performances of the duet were recorded*

die walküre, set of extracts

comprises siegmund comforts sieglinde (orchestral), ride of the valkyries, war es so schmählich and leb wohl du kühnes herrliches kind

camden nj 30 april 1934	philadelphia orchestra davies tibbett	78: victor M 248 78: hmv DB 2470-2473/DB 7953-7956 cd: pearl GEMMCDS 9076 cd: rca/bmg GD 87808 cd: grammofono AB 78766-78767 cd: andante 1130 *GD 87808 contains only leb wohl du kühnes herrliches kind*

other versions of ride of the valkyries and leb wohl du kühnes herrliches kind (wotan's farewell and magic fire music) are listed on the following pages

winterstürme wichen dem wonnemond/die walküre

new york 18 april 1963	american symphony melchior	unpublished recording

wagner/**die walküre, ride of the valkyries**

camden nj may 1920	philadelphia orchestra	victor unpublished
camden nj 25 march 1921	philadelphia orchestra	78: victor 74684/6245 78: hmv 3-0632/DB 387
camden nj april 1921	philadelphia orchestra	victor unpublished
philadelphia 16-18 january 1932	philadelphia orchestra	bell telephone unpublished *two performances were recorded*
philadelphia 29-30 april 1932	philadelphia orchestra	lp: bell telephone laboratories BTL 8001 cd: theo van der burg (netherlands) *recording incomplete*
new york 20-21 april 1961	symphony of the air arroyo, ordassy, yarick, allen, okerson, sarfaty, verrett, parker	lp: victor LM 1336/LSC 2155/VCS 7077/ AGL1-1338 lp: rca RB 16279/SB 2148/GL 11336 lp: camden classics CCV 5005 cd: rca/bmg GD 89293/09026 625972/ 09026 684432/82875 553062
new york 24 january 1964	american symphony	unpublished rehearsal recording
london 26 august 1966	london symphony	lp: decca LK 4851/PFS 4116/SPA 537 lp: london (usa) SPC 21016/SPC 21074/ STS 15565 cd: decca 421 0202/425 7872/433 6392/ 443 9012/475 6090
new york 14 november 1971	american symphony	unpublished recording

wagner/**die walküre, wotan's farewell and magic fire music**

camden nj may 1920	philadelphia orchestra	victor unpublished *may have been magic fire music only*
camden nj april 1921	philadelphia orchestra	victor unpublished *may have been magic fire music only*
camden nj 5 december 1921	philadelphia orchestra	78: victor 74736/6245 78: hmv 3-0723/DB 387 *may have been magic fire music only*
philadelphia 29-30 april 1932	philadelphia orchestra	lp: bell telephone laboratories BTL 8001 cd: theo van der burg (netherlands) *recording incomplete*
philadelphia 9 april 1939	philadelphia orchestra	78: victor 15800 78: victor DB 3942/DB 6024 45: rca camden CAE 101 lp: victor VCM 7101 lp: rca camden CAL 120 cd: pearl GEMMCDS 9076 cd: magic talent MT 48015 cd: magic master MM 37022 cd: phonographe PH 5025-5026 cd: cantus classics 500.090 cd: history 20.3290 cd: andante 1130 *CAE 101 and CAL 120 named performers as warwick symphony orchestra; cantus classics issue incorrectly name the piece as overture*
new york 23 january 1944	nbc symphony	unpublished recording

wagner/walküre wotan's farewell and magic fire music/concluded

new york 17 november 1947	new york philharmonic	78: columbia (usa) M 301 lp: columbia (usa) ML 2153 lp: columbia 33C 1026 lp: columbia (italy) 33QC 1027 cd: theo van der burg (netherlands) cd: cala CACD 0533
houston 30-31 march 1960	houston symphony	lp: everest LPBR 6070/SDBR 3070 lp: world records TP 79 lp: vox STGBY 515040 cd: priceless D 1323X cd: virtuoso 2602 cd: everest EVC 9024
london 30 september 1973	royal philharmonic	unpublished recording
barking 15-19 october 1973	royal philharmonic	lp: rca ARS1-0498 cd: rca/bmg 09026 616682/09026 625972/ 09026 684432/74321 709312/ 82875 553062

WILLIAM WALTON (1902-1983)

partita for orchestra

houston 31 october- 1 november 1960	houston symphony	unpublished recording

spitfire prelude and fugue

new york 6 february 1949	new york philharmonic	cd: wing (japan) WCD 39 cd: theo van der burg (netherlands)

crown imperial, march

geneva august 1973	international youth festival orchestra	unpublished recording

PHILIP WARNER

sinfonietta

new york 4 november 1941	nbc symphony	cd: enno riekena (germany) *first movement only*

BEN WEBER (born 1916)

symphony on poems of william blake

new york 30-31 october 1952	his symphony orchestra galfour	lp: victor LM 1785 lp: composers' recordings CRI 120 cd: citadel CTD 88123 *citadel issue incorrectly dated 1954*

CARL MARIA VON WEBER (1786-1826)

oberon, overture

new york 21 october 1965	american symphony	cd: theo van der burg (netherlands) *this was a rehearsal recording*

perpetuum mobile from the first piano sonata

los angeles 11 august 1946	hollywood bowl symphony stockton, marimba	unpublished recording

invitation to the dance

camden nj 9 may 1919	philadelphia orchestra	78: victor 74598/6237 lp: american stokowski society LSSA 3
philadelphia 2 may 1927	philadelphia orchestra	78: victor 6643 78: hmv D 1285 78: electrola EJ 166 lp: british stokowski society LS 1 cd: biddulph WHL 047 cd: grammofono AB 78552 cd: sirio 530027
philadelphia 4-5 december 1931	philadelphia orchestra	lp: bell telephone laboratories BTL 7901 cd: iron needle IN 1402 cd: theo van der burg (netherlands)

philadelphia 19 april 1940	philadelphia orchestra	78: victor 15189 78: hmv DB 3699 45: rca camden CAE 192 lp: rca camden CAL 123/CAL 282 lp: supraphon 1010 3351-3352 cd: music and arts CD 1173 *rca camden issues naned performers as warwick symphony orchestra; supraphon issue incorrectly dated 1935*
new york 13-17 december 1940	all-american symphony	78: columbia (usa) 11481
new york 9 may 1950	his symphony orchestra	45: victor WDM 1394 lp: victor LM 1083/VIC 1020 lp: hmv ALP 1133 cd: theo van der burg (netherlands)

ANTON VON WEBERN (1883-1945)

passacaglia

philadelphia 16 march 1962	philadelphia orchestra	unpublished recording

KARL WEIGL (1881-1949)

symphony no 5 "apocalyptic"

new york 26-27 october 1968	american symphony	unpublished recording *rehearsal was apparently also recorded*

JAROMIR WEINBERGER (1896-1967)

polka and fugue/schwanda the bagpiper

new york 16 january 1949	new york philharmonic	cd: theo van der burg (netherlands) cd: cala CACD 0537

CHOU WEN-CHUNG (born 1923)

to a wayfarer

new york 3 december 1958	contemporary music society	unpublished recording

HENRI WIENIAWAKI (1835-1880)
violin concerto no 2

los angeles 14 july 1946	hollywood bowl symphony wicks, violin	lp: musenkranz (usa) GMV 13Y

HEALEY WILLAN (1880-1968)
coronation suite

new yotk 16 october 1953	his symphony orchestra westminster choir	cd: enno riekena (germany)

ERMANNO WOLF-FERRARI (1876-1948)
il segreto di susanna, overture

los angeles 16 august 1946	hollywood bowl symphony	unpublished recording

VICTOR YOUNG (1900-1956)
pearls on velvet

los angeles 26 august 1945	hollywood bowl symphony turner	cd: enno riekena (germany)

ERIC ZEISL (1905-1959)
cossack dance

los angeles 18 august 1946	hollywood bowl symphony	unpublished recording

EFREM ZIMBALIST (1889-1985)
american rhapsody

new york 16 january 1944	nbc symphony	unpublished recording

MISCELLANEOUS AND TRADITIONAL

etenraku/japanese ceremonial prelude

camden nj 12 november 18	philadelphia orchestra	78: victor 14142 cd: japanese stokowski society LSCD 20 cd: cala CACD 0501

deep river; doxology

london 19-20 july 1961	new symphony luboff choir	lp: victor LM 2593/LSC 2593 lp: quintessence PMC 7019 cd: rca/bmg 09026 625992/09026 684432

russian christmas music

camden nj 22 october 1934	philadelphia orchestra	78: victor 1692 *recording was re-made in 1939 using the same catalogue number*
new york 19 december 1943	nbc symphony	unpublished recording
new york february 1947	his symphony orchestra	78: victor 11-9837 45: victor 49-0974/ERA 119

veni creator spiritus; veni emanuel

camden nj 7 april 1934	philadelphia orchestra	78: victor 1789 78: hmv DA 1551 cd: japanese stokowski society LSCD 20 cd: cala CACD 0501
new york 29 december 1971	american symphony	unpublished recording